෨ඁ

For Roberta,
    Thank you for all
you do to help others
follow their dreams!
    Continue to follow yours~
        Justina

9/19/14

Justina Lasley's approach to personal growth through dreamwork has been heralded by clients, students and peers:

Justina Lasley has taught countless people how to utilize their dreams in order to bring more happiness, joy, and fulfillment into their lives. Her latest book, Wake Up!, *teaches dreamers how to apply Justina's unique DreamSynergy process to improve their relationships, careers, physical health, and spiritual life. Whether you have just begun to explore your dreams, or you are a seasoned dreamer, this reader-friendly book will teach you something new, something that may change your life.*

—Stanley Krippner, PhD, author, professor at Saybrook University, Fellow of the American Psychological Association

It looks as though Justina Lasley has done it again! Her magisterial Honoring the Dream: A Handbook for Dream Group Leaders, *has become a classic in the field, and by all appearances,* Wake Up! *is poised to take us to a new and exciting level. Justina's DreamSynergy process deepens our understanding of dreams, particularly through a variety of journaling techniques.*

—Jeremy Taylor, DMin, author, professor at Graduate Theological Union, founding member of IASD

As a former Executive Vice President in a Fortune 200 company, and a client of Justina Lasley, I highly recommend her new book, Wake-Up!, *which is a practical guide to the DreamSynergy process that I have experienced first-hand. Justina's knowledge of psychology, symbolism, and archetypes has guided me to understand myself in new ways and to make new decisions that have resulted in major changes in my life.*

—Steve Purdom, MD, retired Executive VP and Board Member of Aflac

This book of Justina's is a precious tool to help dreamers be more at ease with imagery coming from sleep. Justina generously shares her experience and skills to explain what people need to know about dreams in order to pursue their waking life dreams. You will benefit from her expertise, skills, and knowledge about the world of dreams, a fascinating dimension of life.

—Nicole Gratton, author, Founder-Director of École Internationale de Rêves, Montréal, QC

I traveled from Iceland to attend a workshop with Justina. It turned out to be a crucial encounter for me, and in spite of the geographical distance, I enrolled in her program at Institute for Dream Studies in Charleston, SC. It was a leap that brought treasures for my life! I would describe Justina as a midwife who with persistence and a firm hand helped bring forth potential that I had long been aware of but was reluctant to show.

—Hallfríður Ragnheidardottir, poet, IDS-certified dreamworker, Reykjavik, Iceland

This is a truly delightful book on working with your dreams, designed to guide you gently but deeply into your dreams and dream imagery. Wake Up! *provides a broad base of experience for the reader.*

—Bob Hoss, MS, author, Director of DreamScience Foundation, past president of IASD

Justina Lasley brings a wealth of experience, knowledge, and insight to the art of dream interpretation. Through illuminating examples and powerful exercises, she shows you how to awaken your understanding of dream symbols and make constructive changes in your life. Highly recommended.

—Robert Waggoner, author of *Lucid Dreaming: Gateway to the Inner Self*

Justina has developed a process that honors both the dream and the dreamer. Her vast experience, contagious enthusiasm, and gentle approach make her the perfect dream guide. During my time with Justina at the Institute for Dream Studies, I witnessed dramatic transformation in both myself and fellow students. If we all shared our dreams this would be a much healthier, greener and peaceful planet.

—Linda Mastrangelo, MA, certified dreamworker, editor of *Dream News*

Together we applied Justina's method to my dream, and in minutes I found clarity and relief, and I felt empowered by the process. Her DreamSynergy method has proven to be exceptionally efficient for me, compared to my experience with cognitive therapy and other forms of psychological inquiry. I am astonished that my energy could change so positively and so rapidly—within mere minutes—of coaxing out my emotions from what seems like such a simple thing as my dream.

—Ruthanne Miller-Haas, DreamSynergy workshop attendee, New Brunswick, Canada

Justina Lasley is a gifted dream worker. Here she demonstrates that she's a gifted teacher as well. Wake Up! *is one of those rare books with the potential to transform lives. Lasley's exercises and insights about emotions and beliefs are especially powerful aids to self-discovery. Anyone who's committed to awakening the soul's potential and living a meaningful life will find priceless help here!*

—Jean Benedict Raffa, author of *The Bridge to Wholeness, Dream Theatres of the Soul,* and *Healing the Sacred Divide*

In Wake Up!, *Justina Lasley introduces readers to DreamSynergy, a process she has developed to help dreamers understand the symbolic language of their dreams and bring it into consciousness awareness. This book helps us become more fluent in the language of our dreams.*

—Jean Shinoda Bolen, MD, author of *Goddesses in Everywoman* and *Gods in Everyman*

WAKE UP!

Use Your Nighttime Dreams
to Make Your Daytime Dreams Come True

Justina Lasley, MA

BALBOA
PRESS
A DIVISION OF HAY HOUSE

Balboa Press books may be ordered through booksellers or by contacting:

Balboa Press
A Division of Hay House
1663 Liberty Drive
Bloomington, IN 47403
www.balboapress.com
1 (877) 407-4847

Because of the dynamic nature of the Internet, any web addresses or
links contained in this book may have changed since publication and
may no longer be valid. The views expressed in this work are solely those
of the author and do not necessarily reflect the views of the publisher,
and the publisher hereby disclaims any responsibility for them.

The author of this book does not dispense medical advice or prescribe the use
of any technique as a form of treatment for physical, emotional, or medical
problems without the advice of a physician, either directly or indirectly. The
intent of the author is only to offer information of a general nature to help you
in your quest for emotional and spiritual well-being. In the event you use any
of the information in this book for yourself, which is your constitutional right,
the author and the publisher assume no responsibility for your actions.

COVER PHOTO: PETER VAN EVERY "SUNRISE OVER THE LOWCOUNTRY"
AUTHOR PHOTOS: LEIGH HAYWARD www.leighhayward.com

Printed in the United States of America.

ISBN: 978-1-4525-9590-0 (sc)
ISBN: 978-1-4525-9592-4 (hc)
ISBN: 978-1-4525-9591-7 (e)

Library of Congress Control Number: 2014907008

Balboa Press rev. date: 08/25/2014

To Chad
My muse, my nurturer, my support,
my love—my dream come true!

Contents

List of Exercises

Preface

If our dreams are so important, why do so many people ignore them?

Many people don't understand that they can use their dreams to change their lives, and others simply feel that it's just too hard, and it takes too much time and commitment to learn all they need to know in order to pursue their waking life dreams.

Would you like to successfully:

- embrace the person you were born to be?
- find joy in your life beyond your expectations?
- gain insight into yourself and achieve your greatest potential?
- clearly see your life purpose and discover paths to achieving that?
- access realms of spirit and soul similar to those experienced in near-death episodes?
- improve your sleep?

All of us have five or six dreams each night. Many of your life's questions already may have been addressed, but you slept through the answers.

I believe that our dreams are one way God answers our prayers and brings to consciousness our concerns, issues, and questions. Are you listening? Really listening, with an intention of understanding and incorporating the answers into your life?

Our dreams take into account our past experiences, vulnerabilities, and strengths, and can lead us to our future.

Now, what else do you have access to that can do that? We most often look outside of ourselves for answers we actually already have within us. How about that?! Can you believe you already know what you need to do to manifest your waking life dreams and aspirations? Well, you do!

I guarantee that answers are available through your dreams. You just need to learn how to capture and use the information that comes to you each night.

We are off on a great journey. You won't believe what is in store for you in dreamland.

Let's not wait a minute more. Let's move right into what you need to know to Honor Your Dreams—and your life.

☺/☺

So ... WAKE UP! READY, SET, GO!

Acknowledgements

⊚⊚

Cultivate the habit of being grateful for every good thing that comes to you, and to give thanks continuously. And because all things have contributed to your advancement, you should include all things in your gratitude.
—Ralph Waldo Emerson

Where do I begin to thank all my family, friends, and colleagues who have nurtured me to Wake Up! in my life, to work with others to help them move toward their authentic selves, and to have the courage and devote the time to develop this new book?! Although my intention to write the book in three months was not realized, I have enjoyed the long process of reflecting, writing, dreaming, editing, and clarifying the manuscript into the present format, and am forever grateful to all those who encouraged me.

I could not have done this without the help and support of many. *Wake Up!* is definitely a group creation—the synergy of my life, my dreamwork, and the people who have trusted me and supported me. The wisdom and experience of the whole is much greater and more beneficial than anything that I could create on my own.

There are three people in my life who are truly responsible for the book coming to fruition. My amazing, supportive husband, Chad Minifie, felt that there was another book in me. (I, too, thought there was another book—I just didn't think I was up to the mammoth task of writing it.) Chad never lost belief that the book was to be written and published. He used his priestly attributes to listen, nurture, guide, support, and encourage me to continue, even when the writing was tough and other responsibilities interfered with my ability to focus on *Wake Up!* He managed without my attentiveness to house and home, and made sure I got the rest I needed and the time to honor my dreams each morning with my lovingly-delivered cup of tea. He even read and reread the manuscript, carefully and thoughtfully making suggestions. In addition, he is my best publicity agent, always having one of my business cards handy to pass along. I sincerely do not know how he continued to listen to me reflect on the book day after day (and night). I love you, Chad! Thank you.

My dedicated friend Jane Taylor is my "left brain"; she helped me formulate the vision of the book, clarify the process of DreamSynergy™ and prioritize my time to create the book. She hounded me to be precise, to be concise, and to share my story. She was dedicated throughout and gave countless hours to help make this book and my platform accessible to a multitude of people. Not only was she a great help, but so much fun to be with. Thank you, Jane, for fully believing in me and my dreamwork.

I did not fully commit to the idea of writing another book until my previous editor (for *Honoring the Dream*), Mary Thiele Fobian, committed to assisting me. Mary is not only an astute and patient editor, but is also well versed and practiced in dreamwork. I couldn't find a more perfect match to be the co-producer of my final manuscript. Thanks, Mary, for your willingness to take time from your genealogy business to make this book a reality.

My mother, my three daughters (Lasley, Rives, and Abigail), and my son-in law, Andrew, have been very supportive of my efforts. They continually ask me about the book; they show concern whether I am working too hard or not focusing enough on the writing. (Sort of like my dreams: helping to bring balance to my life.) They act as my informal advisors (no problem telling me their honest opinions!), for everything from creative decisions to using technology. I am also grateful to them for providing me with recurring dream characters and for helping me follow my dreams.

My core group of dreaming friends—Corinne Adams, Tallulah Lyons, Paula McInerny, and Emily Woods—entrusted their dreams to me early in my dreamwork, and we continue to share our love of dreams. We support, encourage, and nudge each other to be all that we were born to be.

Each one of the thousands of people I worked with individually— in dream groups, in workshops and at conferences—has added to my understanding of dreams and the power they hold for each of us. If you are one of those people, I sincerely thank you for teaching me by sharing your dreams, and by helping me learn what helps others to understand the meaning of their dreams and to make significant changes in their lives. Thanks for being my test lab and encouraging me to continue my work. Some of those people generously contributed their dreams for *Wake Up!* Thank you, Betsy, Carole, Corinne, James, Jill, Laura, Margaret, Mom, Patti, Peg, Peter, Steve, Sylvia, and Tzivia.

I have an amazing group of supportive friends, especially in Charleston, Atlanta, Lancaster, and Hilton Head Island, who provide the love which allows me to reach out to others. A special thank you to each of them for the love which is woven in and out of the book and my life. One of my friends deserves a special thank you. Susan Dixon Goldsmith, part of our "Magnificent 7," spent countless hours reading the draft and providing important suggestions for clarifying and improving the book for readers who are new to dreamwork. And I thank my friends Peter Van Every and Leigh Hayward Stoudemire for sharing their photography skills.

The International Association for the Study of Dreams has been a constant guide, education, and support for my work in the field of dreams. From my first conference I have been supported and encouraged by many. I would not be at a place where I could write this book without them. Those who were particularly involved in *Wake Up!* include Kelly Bulkeley, Stanley Krippner,

Nicole Gratton, Jeremy Taylor, Lee Irwin, Tallulah Lyons, Bob Hoss, Robert Waggoner, and Peter and Peggy Van Every. The entire team at DreamsCloud (www.DreamsCloud.com) have supported my work and believed in the benefit of my DreamSynergy™ approach.

All of the graduates of my certification course at the Institute for Dream Studies have taught me as much as they have learned. This was a valuable proving ground for my concepts, theories, and exercises, and eventually for development of my DreamSynergy™ process. A very special thanks to each of them for trusting me with their dream education: Laura Baughman, Nanci Curcio, Tzivia Gover, Betsy Grund, Sylvia Green-Guenette, Deborah Hickey, Hallfridur Jakobsdottir, Sharon Kavanaugh, Carrie King, Julie Koewler, Jean McNair, Linda Mastrangelo, Hermine Mensink, Carol Morris, X Parsons, Peggy Raymond, and Sharon Smith-Mathewes.

The education in Transpersonal Psychology I received at the University of West Georgia was significant in moving me along my path and creating a strong foundation for understanding mind, body, and spirit connections. Thank you to all my professors for helping me learn that I didn't need to have the absolute truth (since it seldom exists), and that there is more than one way of knowing. You certainly broadened my understanding of the world and humanity.

Those who helped me to create a platform to support my book have been an important part of the publication process, and I am fortunate to have them on my team. Thank you, Liz Diaz, Suzette and Ben Bussey, Lee Casey, Betsy Grund, and Mary Jo Rotstein.

I received considerable support and guidance from both CreateSpace and Balboa Press in moving through the process of publication. You know who you are. Thank You! I would especially like to thank Flisabeth Deiwart, Sarah Goddard, David Yoder, Staci Kern, Donavan Gerken, Stephanie, Lance, and Stewart.

Springbank Retreat Center is the place that most often has nurtured and supported me in helping others move into their dreams. It is the perfect place to be in union with nature, friendship, unconditional love, and dreams—both waking and sleeping.

Everyone needs a creative space in which to write. I am indebted to Starbucks, Barnes & Noble, and Dunkin' Donuts not only for providing the Chai Tea (non-fat, no water, extra hot), but also for surrounding me with the energy (but not the agendas) of the people I wish to reach.

With nods to the collective unconscious and the energy we share, I am thankful for every dreamer in the world. Each person has contributed to the collective experience of dreaming, and therefore to my dreaming experience and knowledge of the dreaming mind. I hope that we all will wake up to our dreams and move forward in creating the lives we want to live and the world in which we want to live.

My Story

⊚⊚

I must give up what I am in order to become what I will be.
—Albert Einstein

How Dreams Guided Me Back to My Authentic Self and Greatest Potential

As a child I often thought I must have been adopted. Here I was—imaginative and creative and dreamy—all alone in the midst of a very left-brained family interested only in facts and hard-and-fast rules.

My family was well respected in our community, but things look different inside a home than they do from the outside. I felt unseen and unheard so much of my childhood. I took refuge in my room with my dolls. They were always there to listen to me non-judgmentally. I could be myself with them and tell them my deepest secrets. They loved me despite who I saw myself to be—a defective, bad, unpopular, dispensable little girl. When I was sent to my room crying, I would often climb up on some crates in my small closet and write, on tiny strips of paper, about a better way I would live my life when I grew up. Then I would roll the strips tightly, fasten them with Scotch tape so that no one could ever open them, and add them to other paper coils in a secret box.

My mother was there to serve, and the males of the family seemed to be a team who talked about engineering, mathematics, and sports events. I liked to talk about my dolls, play, fantasy—and my dreams. I loved my dreams and thought them amazing, but no one in my family wanted to hear about them, nor did they respect my dreams—or their own. When I ran to the breakfast table, excited about a dream I had, I was frequently told, "Let's talk about something important!"

As an adult, I enjoyed my role as mother, and felt a strong sense of purpose in raising my three daughters. I also enjoyed my volunteer work in Atlanta and being a part of the community there. All of this kept me very busy! But as my daughters grew older and needed my attention less, I had more time to unravel the tightly wound strings of my life (like those tightly wound coils of paper), to begin my search for who I was authentically. I had previously lived my life in a way that would please others, but not necessarily myself. I trusted others' decisions more than my own. I still did not fully believe in my self-worth beyond the value of the roles I played. My purpose no longer was to take care of everyone else's needs, but to open the door to who I was and what I yearned for in my life—to become authentically *Justina*.

I generally was considered successful, well liked, and intelligent, but I felt I was missing something—something that would allow me to live openly, honestly, confidently—and without constant self-criticism and self-judgment.

I always longed to understand more about my family, my friends, and myself: why people did what they did, why I was different, and why I felt so inferior. It didn't matter how much I accomplished, how many friends I had; I always felt that it wasn't enough—that I wasn't enough.

I went to many therapists, read countless self-help books, and attended numerous self-help workshops, always searching, searching for who I was and what I had to offer to this world, and how to live without constant anxiety and self-doubt.

I finally understood in an intellectual way much of what had gone on in my life, in my family, and in my mind. But little changed in the way I perceived myself. I couldn't quit trying to please others. I was constantly trying to find peace with myself.

I missed church on a particular Sunday in 1990, but later I heard that a visiting pastor from California had preached about dreams! "Dreams?! Really? From the pulpit?" Yes!

WOW! I hadn't known that anyone actually believed dreams were important. I thought they were fascinating, but I didn't know that they were filled with wisdom and guidance. I didn't know that my life would change so "dreamatically" when I began to listen to and follow my dreams.

I joined a dream group at the church, led by our interim minister. I remember the first day I shared a dream with the group. I knew I was creative—I had majored in art at Converse College and attended graphics classes at Parsons in NYC—but the dream I shared knocked me off my feet when we began to discuss it and started to find meaning in the images and symbols. Wow! I now realized I was creative in ways I had never imagined. How was I able to create such a fantastic story about my life, and to use metaphors to represent emotions and experiences that I had never before expressed? I suddenly was awed by this avenue called "the dream!"

I had always looked to others for the answers in my life. Before I began to understand—thanks to my dreams—that I possessed my own wisdom, I had sincerely believed that all I needed to do was to figure out what my father would do in a certain situation and then I would have the "right" answer. Really, "the RIGHT answer?" As if anyone has the "right" answer!

In the mid-1990s, at a weekend retreat at the Kanuga Conference Center in North Carolina, Robert Johnson introduced me to the concept of humans having our own innate wisdom. As hard as I tried to understand, it just didn't seem possible to me. One morning I was awakened by the sounds of a bird outside my window. It seemed to be there to help me understand this concept. (Wake Up, Justina!) I had grown up in a family that had high regard for birds and their inherent wisdom. I understood that birds know innately how to live their lives and what they need in order to thrive and be content, but it had never crossed my mind that I could know that for myself! Not me. I had been taught that others always knew what was best for me—that I must always look to my parents, teachers, and elders for instruction and guidance.

As I continued to pay attention to my dreams and share them, my entire existence—the way I saw my world and myself—began to seem different. My experiences and my identity began to make sense, and I began to see my life and myself from a new perspective. I gained confidence and strength to begin to *be* "Justina"—not the Justina who had been defined by others' expectations, but the Justina that God created me to be.

Even as a child, I believed that God understood and cared for me. It was only as an adult that I understood—through my dreams—that I was blessed with incredible gifts, just as we all have our unique gifts. My dreams also clarified that I no longer was being judged constantly—except by myself. My dreams shed light on my past and showed me how it was connected to my present and my future.

By respecting and paying attention to my dreams, I began to recognize and take responsibility for my emotions, my wants, my needs, my hurts, and my truth. My dreams gave me the images that, in turn, gave me the words and the confidence to express my own long-withheld truths. I began to know the little girl who had feared judgment and punishment. I spent time with her in my dreams and in my journal, embracing her and teaching her to trust me to care for her vulnerabilities and fears, and to protect her in ways that I had never been protected.

I found my voice—my authentic voice, not the one I had been taught to use. It felt good. I did face resistance from family and some friends when I became more honest and expressed my needs. It made others uncomfortable. What?! Had I lost my mind? Where was the old Justina, the one who went along with others and never rocked the boat? How did I dare speak the truth when it might make others uncomfortable? Didn't I know that this was disrespectful and unkind?

My dreams never asked me that. They continued to give me courage and honest answers to my questions. They led me to believe in my most spiritual and highest being.

In my dreams I found encouragement to take action in waking life: to go to graduate school, to leave a marriage of twenty-five years that was actually physically killing me, to go alone to study in Paris for the summer, to travel to Russia alone and take the Trans-Siberian Railway to Irkutsk in order to explore and understand my life in its new form, and then to write my first book.

My dreams sustained me as I experienced serious surgeries, chronic illnesses, and injuries. I suffered, but felt continually supported and guided by my dreams. When no one (not even doctors at Emory or Duke medical centers) could diagnose my chronic serious illness, I was blessed with a doctor at my graduate school who was from the Native American culture and was willing to step outside of traditional Western medicine. When he heard about my interest in dreams, he asked me to share some of them with him. On the sanitized paper of the examining table, he drew the images I described of strange amoeba-like shapes crawling up the walls of my childhood bedroom. As he reflected on these images, he was reminded of certain microorganisms and then ordered additional blood work for me. The results of that test led him to identify an extremely low platelet count, which set doctors on the course to eventually diagnose Lupus.

The doctor believed in my dreams and gave me the confidence to continue to follow my dreams as I learned how to cope with Lupus. I went through years of serious complications, but today, with much help and the guidance of my dreams, I am enjoying a life relatively free of symptoms.

Through my dreamwork I learned to trust my intuition. When I traveled to Charleston for a wedding, I intuitively knew that I was "home." I actually purchased my first home alone within a day of arriving. My dreams continued to support that decision as I waited for my new home to be built. This was all so new for me—I had been the person who would visit every possible destination before making the huge decision to leave Atlanta, where I had lived for thirty-five years! I moved to Charleston alone, not knowing why, but believing that I was being guided. I no longer needed to make the "right" decision. I had begun to understand there were no "right" decisions, but that I needed to act on my decisions and move on when they no longer served me. Fortunately, I followed my intuition. Living in the South Carolina Lowcountry has been a blessing in my life—the creativity, spirituality, and genuineness of the people, as well as the beauty and essence of the sea, the sunsets, and the Lowcountry landscape. Two of my daughters even chose to move here, as well. It all supports my work with dreams and the life I choose to live.

My dreams and intuition were instrumental and informative as I met and married Chad Minifie, the man of my dreams. One day I had tearfully shared my previous night's dreams with my very intuitive friend, Cathy. The dreams were brimming with sadness about not having met the man with whom I would share my future. She stopped me, saying she sensed from the dreams that I already had a connection to the man I would marry. As strange as it still seems to me, she was right. I followed her suggestion: I closed my eyes and tried to connect to that love I yearned for. I quickly felt connected to both New England and England, which seemed very bizarre. I didn't know many people in New England and had never spent time there (except brief visits to my youngest daughter when she was a student at Bates College in Maine), and I had no connections to England and had not visited there in thirty-five years.

The feeling of that experience stayed with me for several weeks. After a month or so, on e-Harmony (How can it be?!), I met a man who lived in Hilton Head Island, and decided to meet him for dinner in Charleston. Soon after being seated, we began discussing background that was more personal than e-Harmony had allowed. I asked, "Where are you from originally?" I am still in awe of his answer: "Well, I have spent most of my life in New England, but my family comes from England." I almost fainted. Of course, I didn't tell him about my intuitive experience until we had dated for several months. I didn't want him to think I was "crazy." I still am hesitant to even tell you this story because it seems so unlikely. But it's true, and the experience expanded my view of what is possible, and connected me in an even deeper way to my dreams and visions.

Through my dreamwork, I let go of the fear that controlled my life and I felt more confident in my decisions and myself. I knew that I was living my authentic life, becoming all that I was born to be, and finding purpose in my life that felt God-guided. That again was partly through a remarkable and memorable dream in which I heard the voice of God calling my name and showing me the way.

Justina's Dream: He's Calling My Name
Emotions: ok, good, awed, anxious, afraid

My oldest daughter and I are looking for a place to build a vacation home. We're on a day trip to look for it. We arrive in a little community and find an area that looks good. In the distance we see a huge rocky mountain jag. It's unbelievably beautiful—just rises right out of otherwise fairly flat land. The mountain is very tall and steep. It's a tall triangular form. It's somewhat golden in color and sort of crystal-like in shape.

My daughter and I are sitting on the curb on the side of the road. I hear my name—"Justina"—called out softly and evocatively. I look around, and across the street I see some people sitting in rocking chairs on the porch of an old white house. One of the men sitting on the porch nods to me, indicating that he's the one who has spoken.

Quietly he comes across the street and leads me into a church behind the area where I'm sitting. He says it would be a good place to build my house. I'm very confused because the church is standing there. He says that they are restoring the church. A team of men are actually disassembling the church piece-by-piece. They're taking pieces of wood off the ceiling, etc. It will all be put back in a similar manner after paint, etc., is taken off. I'm totally confused about how I can build my house here if the church is already on the lot. The man doesn't seem confused at all.

ॐ

This dream has been a guiding light on my path toward working in the field of dreams. I have felt called to this work, and this dream supported that feeling. It has been important to me as a transformative dream. I knew upon waking that the dream had significance in my life journey. I will never forget the sound of the man calling my name. To this day (seventeen years later), it is very calming and comforting to me. The voice and manner of the man who guides me seem to convey the aura of the Divine.

The dream showed me that I am to build my place in a restored church—not in the church of the past, but the church of the future. It is a church that will be taken apart and put back together in an improved way. In the dream I fight the suggestion and look for an easier way.

The crystal shape and the golden color of the mountain in the dream feel important and carry archetypal energy for me. There has always been a deep, spiritual aspect to my dreamwork. When I question the path of work I have chosen, I am encouraged to continue on my spiritual path by this and other powerful dreams.

Archetypes

Underlying patterns that form the basic blueprint for the major dynamic components of the human personality. Examples include Mother, Father, Devil, Divine Child, Goddess, Lover, Wise One, etc.

Carl Jung explains the archetype as "an inherited tendency of the human mind to form representations of mythological motifs—representations that vary a great deal without losing their basic pattern." Archetypes are part of our inheritance as members of the human race.

I learned to let go of other people's judgments and projections and to understand that by following the wisdom of my dreams, I was following an authentic path to my true Self, the path that I was born into this world to follow. My dreams guided me to work through issues with my parents and create a more loving, honest, and open relationship with them. I am forever grateful to them for being willing to go through my process of individuation with me, no matter how difficult it was for us. We loved each other enough to not give up easily on accepting each other in our new relationship. I couldn't have done it without the support and guidance of my dreams.

My life is happier and more joyful and fulfilling than ever. I still question, I still want to know why, and I still yearn to be all that is in my potential. I won't give up and neither will my dreams. They are always with me, beckoning me, nudging me, instructing me, and guiding me. I will always treat them with the respect and attention they deserve.

My self-image has changed. I have new confidence in my worth and abilities. I find wisdom within myself. I look inward much more than I look outward. I am finally a priority in my life. Along with my work in dreams, I have been in therapy, but I give my dreams much of the credit for encouraging me to undertake the changes I have made. Dreams gave me the images, the vision, and the practice to become the woman that God intended me to be. I am not finished, and neither are my dreams. Change is a lifelong process that I welcome and embrace.

I am dedicated not only to my dreams and their messages, but also to helping *you* access this magnificent gift of dreams. I feel that the world would be a gentler, wiser, more accepting place if we *all* would pay attention to our dreams. If God speaks to us—and I believe He does—then I believe that dreams are His language. We are born with this incredible ability to stay connected to the One who created us, but we toss our dreams aside as if they are frivolous and meaningless. We were given this ability to stay connected to our essence, our true authentic essence, yet we give more value to our waking thoughts and decisions.

This gift is extremely important. I want to show you ways to begin to understand and embrace the wisdom of your dreams, and to make it easy and even fun for you. I want to connect you to your inner wisdom.

Justina's Dream: Glossing Over the Past
Emotions: ok, disgusted, mad

I'm in the living room of my childhood home. A crew of men has just finished painting all the walls. I am surprised by the colors. I question them and the painters say it's easier to just paint without asking. The head guy says they'll be glad to repaint with another color if we don't like this one.

The breakfast room, as well as the living room, has a wall that is Pepto pink. Also some powder pink trim. The ceiling of the living room is painted a dark gray—so is a wall. Another wall is yellow.

I show the walls to Mom and she is not really upset. I can't believe it—they are awful.

It all looks terrible. The paint is awful colors and it's a poor painting job—very shiny and everything just painted over. I wonder why Mom isn't really upset?! Guess I shouldn't cause a problem if she doesn't think it's a problem.

❧

This was a graphic metaphor of the life I lived growing up and that my dreams have led me to understand and deal with. As a child I noticed that things were not right, but no one else seemed to notice or care. I often felt crazy when I mentioned things to my mom. She survived by the grayness of her life—not feeling, not being hurt, not letting her emotions overtake her ability to function. Everything was "glossed over," as in the dream.

The Pepto pink reminds me of the medicine we took when we had stomach-aches, which was often in our family. After all, we were all hiding from the truth that surrounded us. The yellow reminds me of the fear I lived with daily—fear of being punished for being *me.* I don't know why yellow elicits fear from me, but it does. This is why it's important to create your personal dream dictionary—your associations to a particular color may be different from others' associations.

Even though I have spent years working through the pain of the mistreatment I felt, I still have dreams that give me support to continue my growth, and to help others who experienced abuse as children.

☺/☺

Wake Up! ... and come along with me.

CHAPTER 1

⊚⊚

Wake Up to Your Life and Your Dreams

The true spiritual secret is this: What you seek, you already are. True success is discovering your inner divinity—it's the ability to love and have compassion, trust your intuition, and awaken to your unlimited creative nature.

—Deepak Chopra

Were you ever wakened by a nightmare that left you breathless? Do you have recurring dreams that won't go away? Have you ever wakened from an emotional dream packed with crazy images and wondered, "What was *that* about?!"

Well, you're not alone! Dreams intrigue people in all cultures. Throughout history, artists, scientists, musicians, poets, and writers have reaped great value from their dreams. They have used their dreams to invent things, solve problems, and create musical and artistic masterpieces that enrich our lives today. Jean-Jacques Rousseau, Georg Friedrich Handel, Thomas Alva Edison, and Robert Louis Stevenson all used their dreams to get in touch with their most creative selves. Many of William Blake's engravings have a dreamlike quality, and the method he used for his engravings was revealed to him in a dream. Renowned scientist August Kekule discovered the ringed structure of the benzene molecule after daydreaming about a coiled snake biting its own tail.

In dreams your concepts become clearer. It is difficult, if not impossible, to reach such a high level of creativity and awareness in your waking life. Edison found his dreams quite useful. He once dreamed of a lamp that could be operated by electricity, and despite thousands of failures he believed in that dream and used it as his muse until he brought the first electrical light into the world.

You may not have aspirations to become a famous painter or musician, or to create a world-changing invention, but whatever your hopes and daytime dreams may be, your nighttime dreams can help you understand and overcome obstacles that stand between you and your goals.

> *If we all did the things we are capable of, we would astound ourselves.*
>
> —Thomas Alva Edison

Golfer Jack Nicklaus overcame a major decline in his winnings with the help of a dream. In the following dream he discovered a new way to hold his golf club, which he credits to improving his golf game:

> *Wednesday night I had a dream and it was about my golf swing. I was hitting them pretty good in the dream and all at once I realized I wasn't holding the club the way I've actually been holding it lately. I've been having trouble collapsing my right arm taking the club head away from the ball, doing it perfectly in my sleep. So when I came to the course yesterday morning I tried it the way I did in my dream and it worked. I shot a sixty-eight yesterday and a sixty-five today.*
>
> —Jack Nicklaus

Let's take a quick look at some important aspects of dreams.

Dreams are a natural, healthy part of our human existence.
All humans and most animals dream each night—and perhaps also when they are awake. (Researchers are beginning to regard this as a probability.) There are few things that all of us do every day without intention, but some functions that take place through no effort on our part are vital: we breathe, our hearts beat, our cells rejuvenate. And no matter how we evolve, we continue to dream. As hard as we might try, we cannot will ourselves *not* to dream.

Dreams come to all of us every night. It may be hard to believe, but you have five to six dreams each night. It's not a matter of whether you *dream*, but whether you *remember* your dreams. Various things affect the dreaming mind—sleep patterns, medications, and illness—but generally your mind is providing you with wisdom and great entertainment each night.

Dreams originate in parts of your brain that become active when you sleep. They come from your unconscious mind, which contains innate wisdom, immense creativity, suppressed memories, and hidden desires. You do not have access to your unconscious when you are awake (except through specific techniques such as hypnosis). Everything in your unconscious is "beneath the surface," but still exerts a great influence on your behavior. Your unconscious contains both personal and collective knowledge.

Unconscious

The unconscious is part of the mind which contains our feelings, desires, thoughts, and memories that are outside of our waking conscious awareness. Sigmund Freud taught that the unconscious has great influence on our behavior and experience, despite our lack of awareness. Unconscious material is often revealed in dreams.

Dreams have played an important role throughout history and across the globe. In many ancient civilizations, dreams informed decision-making for both the individual and the community. In certain cultures, dreams continue to provide the foundation of collective wisdom.

A profound example of the modern use of dreams by a native culture is found deep in the Amazon rainforest, where the Achuar people have thrived for centuries. They remained isolated from "modern culture" until the 1990s, when Achuar elders dreamed regularly of imminent threats to their community. Dreams brought to their awareness the corporate exploitation of nearby communities and land.

Dreams also have been credited with subsequently leading the Achuar and dreamers in the United States into an alliance, led by Lynne and Bill Twist. By exploring the best of modern and traditional cultures, the Pachamama Alliance has successfully implemented solutions for preservation and native self-governance. Today, for the Achuar and many in the United States, dreams provide a vision for survival that involves balancing modern and traditional aspects of culture.

Visit www.pachamama.org to learn more about the Achuar people and the Pachamama Alliance.

Dreams are spiritual guides that lead us to our innate wisdom. Many people believe that dreams contain messages from God or a Higher Power, and that they offer answers to our prayers. Many place great value on knowing that they do not need to go through an intermediary (for example, a priest or minister) to hear and obtain true spiritual wisdom.

Justina's Dream: Beautiful White Flowers in Holy Land
Emotions: awed, serene

I'm on a tour of a "special land" with a group. No one is supposed to touch anything—the land and things there are all very holy. We pass a field of small white flowers. The flowers have just begun to bloom. I notice their root systems are runners and spread out just above the ground, like rhizomes. I did not previously know that particular root system was how the beautiful flowers spread and multiplied.

The reference to holy land gave me a spiritual feeling. The runners of the plants seemed to relate to my dreamwork's manner of growth. It reminded me that my work needed to spread rather visibly above ground (as an extrovert), with my main roots reaching underground (as an introvert). I also realized that it is different from the way a potato might grow underground (as an introvert). I knew that it was important for me to continue to reach out to the multitude by influencing individuals who could, in turn, reach others through dreamwork.

Dreams provide support as you change and grow. Dreams allow you to go through personal changes at your own rate, taking into account your past and present. No outside source can offer you this unique vision. Your dreams are tailor-made to match your personal way of understanding and changing.

Dreams inform us and lead us to new understanding. Dreams offer you new information each night. Dreams do not come to tell you what you already know (although they often use what you already know to lead you to an understating of what you do not know). Please don't ignore a dream because it seems to offer only a simple synopsis of the previous day. There is new information for you in this dream; otherwise your psyche would not have presented it.

> **Psyche**
> The Greeks envisioned the psyche as the soul or the very essence of life. In this book, the term "psyche" refers to the entirety of "the mind," encompassing everything that is conscious and unconscious.

Dreams are personal. It is not always easy to accept that your dreams are all about *you*. I know it would be easier if they were all about other people's problems. It's not difficult to see clearly what *other people* need to do to make their lives better, but your dreams focus on *your* life and personal growth!

Dreams tell us the truth. This one aspect of dreams may impact you greatly if you have lived your life without recognizing the difference between your own truth and someone else's truth. Your dreams will support your well-being and your desire to make your life better.

Dreams help us move toward our authentic nature. Do you sense that you were born with a purpose, but feel that you have not realized that potential? By guiding you toward a greater understanding of who you are and a fuller recognition of what you want, your dreams help you move toward fulfillment.

 Dreams bring balance to our personalities. Do you sometimes get out of balance with work, play, or rest? Your psyche likes them all, but wants you to have balance. Your dreams will help you adjust. If you become too involved in work, and neglect rest and play, your dreams will speak up and suggest a redirection.

Justina's Dream: Locked in Bedroom
Emotions: anxious, afraid, frustrated

Bea realizes that we are locked in my bedroom. At first I think it will be easy to escape, but she points out that we don't have our purses with us; therefore, we have no cell phone or keys. We need a key to unlock the door and all our numbers to call are in our cell phones.

There is a rotary dial phone on side table. I think I can remember Mom's number. I try to dial, but it is difficult because it's dark and I can't see the numbers on the phone. I keep misdialing. I remember a friend's number enough to try but it's difficult to dial—I can't get it. I don't know what we'll do.

In waking life, I was exhausted from entertaining company for a week, but didn't realize quite how badly I felt until a day later—I woke up full-fledged SICK. My body knew it needed to be locked in my bedroom for rest, but I didn't yet quite believe that it was okay for me to cancel all of my obligations. I wish I had heeded the call the morning of my dream and stayed in bed; perhaps then I would not have been so sick later! Another thing that should have been a hint was that I was locked in with Bea, who has been such a caretaker, helper, and nurturer for me. Usually when she appears in my dreams, I know I seek nurturance. I needed to activate that part of myself.

Dreams come only when we are capable of dealing with the message. Your dreams will not lead you down paths that you are not prepared to navigate. Do not worry; your psyche seems to be self-regulating, allowing information to emerge from your unconscious only when you have the strength and ability to deal with it. You may not want to deal with it—it may require a lot of effort and energy—but you can do so, and your well-being will actually benefit greatly when you follow your dreams' guidance!

Dreams are patient and persistent. You may have had good teachers and mentors in the past, but you never have had, and never will have, a teacher as patient and persistent as your dreams. They come to you every night. They repeat themselves until you get the message and take action to change a negative situation. And they don't shout out unless you refuse to pay attention—in which case they can get really tough and give you a taste of the risks and consequences that could result from not heeding their guidance.

Dreams speak to us in symbolic and metaphoric language. People ask me, "If dreams are so important, why aren't they easier to understand?!" I'm sure you've heard the phrase, "A picture is worth a thousand words." And you probably are aware that many religious figures spoke in parables. Images and concepts can convey multiple levels of meaning and emotional impact. You can interpret a picture or a parable in a way that is highly personal and meaningful to you. Symbols and metaphors can contain unending meaning for you.

Judith's Dream: Clarify
Emotions: happy

I am sitting in a coffee shop having a meeting with my pastor. I tell him I want to do some kind of work with members of our congregation to help individuals tell their life stories, particularly the difficult stories, and to find a way to help them heal these stories. I give examples of different ideas like using guided imagery to go back into the memory, tell their stories to others, and look at Biblical stories to see if they have any similarities to their own story. I feel kind of confused when I try and explain what I want to do, but I really have a passion for doing something like this. My Pastor looks directly at me and says, "I think this may be something worth looking into, but you need to clarify how you want to go about it."

I woke up feeling very excited about this dream and it was fresh in my mind for days. Three days later I met a woman who shared a table with me in a restaurant. I learned that she was a professor and her area of interest is helping individuals write their memoirs. That sparked more interest in the project.

Over the course of a couple months I was consumed with learning everything I could about helping people to write their spiritual autobiographies and to heal through story. Now, eight months later, another pastor and I are piloting a class about "Remembering and Telling your Story." We are hoping to expand this to be a church-wide program for members of all ages.

I feel that this was a call from God that appeared in my dream. The dream helped me put into words something I had thought about before on some level and gave me the courage to "clarify" my intention and go forward with a plan for a working model.

Dreams are not confined to our concepts of time and space. There are no limits in your dreams, no restrictions about where you can be, who you can be with (dead or alive), or what languages you can speak. You can fly, climb a 10,000-foot mountain, be both child and adult simultaneously, and stand in a structure that existed only in the past.

Dreams educate us about emotions. Emotions are very important in our personal journey—causing us to go forward in the process of change, or resist it. In my view, emotions are part of the "gold" we mine from the dream. They teach you about how you act and why you do the things you do. In our fast-paced world, you may lose sight (or feeling) of your emotions. You may not even know how you feel, and in fact you may camouflage your emotions so that you don't feel anything—or so you may believe! Most often our actions and decisions are based on emotions; if you don't even know what those emotions are, you may be making decisions that do not support your needs.

You can make amazing progress toward making your waking-life dreams come true by identifying, claiming, and processing the emotions that are emphasized in your nighttime dreams.

Dreams help us cope with loss. This support sometimes goes beyond dealing with emotional responses to loss. Dreams can illuminate the many practicalities involved (for example, what steps we need to take), and help in the process of adopting a new perspective on life when are faced with letting go of that one special person, pet, object, belief, or addiction.

Mom's Dream: I Can No Longer Follow
Emotions: ok, afraid, sad, accepting

I am walking down a dirt road and see a man dressed in an overcoat and fedora hat. I am following him. I want to yell out to him, but he is too far away. I continue to follow, but come to a chasm in the road. There is no way I can get across the huge, dark opening in the land. I see him continue and know that I cannot go.

My mom had this dream soon after my father died. They were married for over seventy years and she was usually by his side. The chasm illustrated clearly that she could not follow him now in his transition.

The dream had a calming effect on Mom. The dream provided her with supportive, quiet energy. It presented her with an understanding that this was the way things were, and that there was nothing to do and no reason to be alarmed. The overcoat and fedora reminded her of Dad, and the road seemed like the ones they often drove, in their hobby of finding a quiet country road they had never traveled. The dirt road also may have represented a primal path that we all take—ashes to ashes/dust to dust—as opposed to a man-made thoroughfare in a populated place.

Dreams that recur are especially important. Recurring dreams often drive people to seek help in understanding their dreams. A recurring dream is evidence that your psyche is trying to deliver an extremely important message—so important that it repeats the dream (or dream image) until you hear the message. You may grow annoyed and think, "I have been dreaming this same dream for years and I can't stand it anymore. I have to know why!" As mentioned before, dreams are patient, but if there comes a time when you are not paying attention, dreams will aggravate you by giving you the same message over and over.

Dreams in the form of nightmares come as a "wake-up" call. In the same way that recurring dreams annoy us, nightmares frighten us into taking action. Nightmares are neither good nor bad, but are dreams that carry important information for you. They literally wake you up to the fears that may be preventing you from moving forward in your life. They contain time-sensitive material that should be dealt with immediately if you don't want to suffer consequences in your waking life. The message has most likely been coming through your dreams for months or even years with no result. As you begin to pay close attention to your recurring dreams and nightmares, you will learn to hear the subtle message without them waking you in tears or a cold sweat!

Dreams are an important indicator of physical and psychological health. You may first be alerted to a physical or psychological problem or solution by a dream. Listening to dreams will teach you to listen carefully to your body. Remember that dreams speak in symbolic language, and that a particular problem or solution presented in a dream should not necessarily be interpreted literally. More often they will be represented in a metaphorical way.

My dream of poisonous snakes released from a Dirt Dauber nest showed me how to release the poison from my then-degenerating hand—a hand that even well-known physicians had not been able to heal.

I had been dealing with Lupus for quite some time when I fell and injured my hand; the Lupus caused complications. (Lupus is a disease that causes the body to receive the wrong messages and instead of healing the injury, the body turns on itself. How appropriate for someone with a life history of self-sabotage.) I consulted several doctors at Duke Medical Center, as well as "the best hand surgeon in the country" in Atlanta. No one in the medical community knew how to stop the deterioration of my hand. I was sent to physical therapy and was finally helped to some extent by acupuncture. The following dream is what provided information for a major turn-around in my healing.

Justina's Dream: Extracting Snakes from Dirt Dauber's Nest
Emotions: amazed, awed, nervous

A woman notices a nest of some kind on the door handle inside the car. I am in the passenger seat and the nest is on my door. She says it has to come out. She doesn't alarm me, but says she will get it out. She carefully takes the clay nest off the door and examines it. It looks like a Dirt Dauber's nest. I think how dangerous this could be. She seems very capable of doing it.

She carefully puts the nest under water in a sink. She then breaks off the tip of one of the nest's tubes and cautiously pulls out a poisonous snake (rattlesnake). She adeptly and consciously breaks the neck of the snake by flicking it with her fingers. She continues to repeat the process with each of the nest's tubes until all the poisonous snakes have been destroyed.

I am very nervous about it all, but she is very calm and focused.

℘

The dream had a quiet, spiritual presence about it. When I woke up, it seemed very important.

While describing the Dirt Dauber's nest to a dream group, I realized that it resembled the fingers of a human hand! I was shocked! I had seen many Dirt Dauber nests in my life, but I had never realized that it so closely resembled a human hand. It was even similar to the color of my hand! I was in awe, knowing that this dream might offer healing guidance for my very painful injured finger and hand.

I told my physical therapist about the dream on my next visit and she immediately said, "What a great idea. We just got a new water therapy that I want to try on you!" The therapy was done by submerging my hand underwater and applying a controlled electrical impulse to it. It helped!

I also did visualization several times a day—imagining that I was pulling the poison out of my fingers, just as the wise woman did in the dream. It was an amazing healing process.

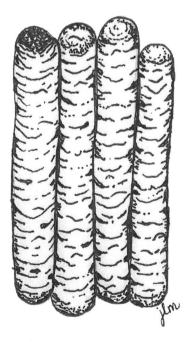

Dirt Dauber's nest as seen in dream

Justina's Dream: Don't Want to Reconnect
Emotions: irritated

I need to call the Gas/Electric Company to turn the power back on, since we have just returned from vacation. I don't really want to, so maybe I won't. I don't really want to reconnect!

∽

We had just returned from three weeks of vacation in New Hampshire, where we had had no agenda or obligations. I feared being caught back up in my "real" world and not having the quiet time that I had grown to love in the mountains. The dream reminded me to be careful to protect and continue the reflective time I had experienced while vacationing, and not to "turn the power back on and reconnect" too quickly. I knew that my past behavior would have been to jump back in to catch up for time "lost."

Wake Up! to your dreams … because paying attention to your nighttime dreams will help you make your daytime dreams come true. Dreams have been doing this for centuries and in all cultures. Trust them. You will be very glad when you do!

Chapter 2

⊚⊚

Change Your Life through Dreamwork

If one advances confidently in the direction of his dreams, and endeavors to live the life which he has imagined, he will meet with a success unexpected in common hours.

—Henry David Thoreau

Change and Personal Growth

You will not change simply because someone else wants that change. Personal growth will not take place until you are ready. Even when we want to change and are ready, doing so is difficult. For those of you who are open and ready, the dream is an excellent catalyst for this process. The dream softens and eases the work of transformation.

The Urge to Change

Why do people want change? You may simply be unhappy with life as it is. You may believe an alteration in behavior is the best way out of the situation. At this point, you may have spent years trying to change the other people in your life with little or no success.

I remember the day that this fundamental concept became clear to me: If others in my life were not going to change, perhaps I was going to have to alter *my* behavior! When I started individual therapy, I was amazed that it had taken me so long to figure out that I could focus on making my own life better. I had spent an unbelievable amount of energy, time, and expense trying to convince others to see my viewpoint. The walls of confusion and frustration came down brick by brick when I assumed responsibility for my own behavior. The insight necessary to initiate this change was generated by dreamwork and movement toward the person I was intended to be.

Dissatisfaction

Most people seek change when they are dissatisfied with the way things are working—or not working—in their lives. You may want to improve your relationships, career, or health. The dream is a wonderful vehicle for this type of change because it is not concerned with other people's behavior. The dream is concerned only about the welfare of the dreamer—that is YOU!

Loss

One is forced to live differently when circumstances are altered through the death of a child or spouse, divorce, career loss, financial upheaval, or a health issue. It is certain that the loss will cause change; it is up to the individual whether it is a positive or negative change.

Unfortunately, you might quickly replace what you lost: spouse, job, home, etc. You may cover up the pain and anxious feelings, thereby losing an opportunity for personal growth and change. Fear might cause you to move right back onto familiar ground. You may use busy-ness, alcohol/drugs, or "toys" to move away from the tension that you feel. You might stay stuck in your pain, living the remainder of your life in denial and depression. It is difficult to face the pain of loss and move through it to new, more positive ways of being, but oh, it's so worth the difficulty.

Spiritual Awakening

Some people may have a spiritual awakening as the result of a life event—a death, a birth, a medical diagnosis, a psychic experience. This special event may have moved you to a deep awareness of your spiritual nature. Consciousness of the Divine is often present. Your senses are heightened and you see the world differently than you did before the awakening. It can be an experience of transcendence or one of being unusually grounded and centered.

The spiritually awakened person finds that nothing seems as it was and cannot live life as he/she has in the past. If you have experienced such an occurrence, you may not share the event with anyone for fear of being misunderstood or considered crazy. The event is of such importance, and contains so much emotion and awe for you, that you don't want to risk having someone belittle it.

Often dreams become more intense and recall is greater after a spiritual awakening. They seem to reflect the importance of the event and honor the dreamer's experience. An individual who previously had no interest in delving into the dream world may now feel a strong urge to find meaning in his dreams.

Connie's Angel Dream
Emotions: blissful, peaceful, awed

I am walking home through a beautiful open field. The sky is pale yellow. There's a long wooden boardwalk across the field—and a grove of trees far off to the right. The sky is full of clouds, and it is daytime. I am very peaceful and happy because it's so lovely. I look at the clouds and watch them move, thinking I could do this all day. Suddenly, one of the moving clouds turns into an angel which swoops down. I am stunned and excited. We point at each other (like the Sistine Chapel!). Then, as I am lying on the ground, face up, another angel swoops down with big feathery wings and flutters his/ her wings all over me like a blanket. It is a spiritual moment in the field. Angels are everywhere.

⌒

The angel dream (angels covering me up in a field) has supported me in an amazing way throughout my journey with cancer. I really felt the depth, breadth, and movement of the angels' wings on me in a palpable way—and this assurance has been repeated in many other ways. When I was in Nicaragua—twice—I was physically smothered and lifted up in prayer by two different groups of people. It felt exactly like the angels returning. I knew the feeling and emotions, and so the experience wasn't scary—it was mystical and life-giving [and] I felt God was reminding me of His care and presence. Now, whenever I see a feather—even a bird feather on a walk—I think of the angel. This dream is a wonderful metaphor for my faith, past and present.

Personal Growth

Robert Kegan's graphic representation of personal growth as a spiral movement is helpful in understanding the process of change. We start at the bottom of the spiral, making positive changes in our lives. We come to several snags—core issues—in the process as we move around the first level of the spiral. With effort and new awareness we are able to move beyond the difficult places.

As you continue in your individuation process, you move into the second level of the spiral. Again you hit the snags. You might feel as if you have made no progress, and might say, "Gosh, I am right back where I was a year ago."

Core Issue

A central and major psychological matter that usually derives from childhood experiences and deters a person from moving forward in personal growth.

Carolyn's Dream: Getting Caught in Thorns Again
Emotions: glad, anxious, curious, frustrated, angry, afraid, determined

I'm in a semi-urban area with three female friends, surrounded by high rises and parks. We walk on the sidewalk. It's a sunny, pleasant day. Everything seems especially clear and bright.

At a street corner, a bench and chair sit next to planters filled with colorful flowers. Instead of sitting and enjoying the day, I lead my friends down a few steps to get to the street, and I feel prickles around my ankles – there are thorns in the plants. We decide to investigate a basement apartment with worn stone steps almost hidden by shrubs. I lead the group down and find a partially hidden door. I'm grabbed by more prickles and thorns, and as I turn to go back up the thorns are everywhere, reaching out to grab me. I feel the pain of the thorns. I reach up, trying to part them so I can get through. I'm determined to endure the pain of getting free.

ॐ

I had been in this place of thorns many times throughout my life. Why did I always take myself down when things were looking good for me and all was bright for my future? The dream was a wakeup call, and a gift, in acknowledging my greatest strengths – willpower and determination. I knew that I was going to have to allow myself to feel the pain of my loss, and now I was determined to face losses of the past in a way that freed me from being caught back up in the sadness.

Then I thought of another possibility—that as part of my journey into wholeness I was being drawn to explore the hidden places, the prickles and thorns of my life. In this dream I only get to the outskirts of the deep work, but I acknowledge my willpower and determination to assemble the tools I'll need.

The truth is that you are not at the same place where you were earlier. Examine the predicament in waking life and compare your reaction to it *now* to your reaction *in the past*. Usually, you can see (sometimes with help) that you have not become as depressed as before, have not stayed with the problem as long, or have found new solutions to the problem that you had never recognized before.

Each time another level of the growth spiral is reached, you may hit the same snags. At each level obtained, you will know new ways to deal with the problem.

With awareness, you do change! You seldom go back to exactly the way you were before honoring your dreams and their truth.

Justina's Dream: Packing Light
Emotions: glad, pleased with self

I am going somewhere. I have a small black bag with me. I know it is amazing that I've packed so light for such a long trip. I am very proud of myself.

Over the past years, I have had recurring dreams of packing and not being able to get it all in the suitcase and never finishing. Everyone else is ready to depart and I am still trying to gather everything and not hold others up. It's usually endless and unsuccessful.

This dream showed me that I had made progress in the area of preparing for an event or trip and not being overwhelmed by too much stuff (too many tasks and details.) I felt very responsible, calm and organized in the dream. The dream reinforced new behavior for me. Maybe the snag won't be so big for me next time!

How the Dream Facilitates Change

One of our dreams' purposes is to bring what is unconscious into consciousness, yet the dreamer is often unaware that she is going into a vulnerable area. In therapy, as you get close to an issue, you may choose to move away from it out of fear. We all are adept at avoiding deep issues that require difficult change. But the dream has the power of story and metaphor; it catches us unaware. We don't really know where it is taking us; therefore we may go to places we normally would not choose to go. This is part of the power and magic of the dream.

Awareness

The prerequisite to personal change and transformation is awareness. Until you are aware of your desire to change, your need to change, and your sabotaging behaviors, you cannot make positive change! First comes awareness, then decisions based on that awareness lead to the changes you would like to make in your relationships, finances, career, and health. So *Wake Up!* in your daily waking life. Remember that how you live your day is how you live your life! Practice awareness in every moment of your day; tune in to your life and your dreams.

To practice new awareness, try the following dream exercise. All you need is one object. And if you don't yet remember a dream, just get comfortable, close your eyes and let your mind wander. What image or object comes to mind? Use that as your representative object.

Exercise: The Image Speaks

This exercise is one of my favorites for reaching an "aha" within a few minutes. It makes a strong impact in a short amount of time. I adapted the exercise from one Bob Hoss (author of *Dream Language: Self-Understanding through Imagery and Color*) shared with me.

1. Choose an image (object, animal, etc.) in the dream to which you are drawn.
2. Close your eyes and see the image. Imagine that you are walking around the object and look at it closely; imagine touching the object.
3. Once you are familiar with the image, move into becoming that image. Believe that you are that image, playing the role of that image on a stage.
4. What do you look like? What do you feel like?
5. Open your eyes and complete the following sentences, as if you are the image.

   I am _____ (the image/object).
   As _____ (the image/object), my purpose is _____.
   As _____ (the image/object), I like _____.
   As _____ (the image/object), I dislike _____.
   As _____ (the image/object), I feel _____.
   As _____ (the image/object), I fear _____.
   The most important thing about me is _____.
   What I want most is _____.

6. It will be helpful to read this aloud—even if to yourself. Substitute your own name for the first sentence (for example, "I am Ben"). Then read each sentence as "I am Ben and my purpose is _____," substituting the answers you wrote for the image.
7. Now reflect on your waking life and consider whether one or more of the statements fits a current situation you are experiencing.
8. Do the "I like" and "I dislike" statements sound like a conflict or argument going on in your head?
9. Does the fear expressed in the "I fear" statement prevent you from moving forward in your personal growth? Does that statement prevent you from acquiring "What I want most"?

John used kudzu as the image from his dream. Kudzu is a very fast-growing vine.

I am John.
My purpose is to help people breathe easier (by creating oxygen).
I like to grow fast.
I dislike being cut back.
I feel that I am misunderstood and have little respect from others.
I fear being killed off.
The most important thing about me is that I connect things as I spread.
I want most to be allowed to grow and spread; and to be respected.

John saw more clearly that his personal growth was important to support others in their growth. His desire to reach out and touch others' lives was affirmed. He reflected in his journal how and why he often felt misunderstood and disrespected. John also realized that he often expected his personal growth to be too fast.

Intention and Commitment

If you don't remember your dreams right away, don't give up. Continue expressing your intention and committing to the process until you remember a dream. Remember: Commitment is essential to your success in dreamwork.

Your dreams will inspire, guide, and encourage you. But think about how you would like to use your dreams. Why do you want to set your intention to remembering your dreams, and make a commitment to understanding the messages of your dreams? What is your goal for your dreamwork?

Check the areas that are important to you at this time in your life:
- ☐ I want to get to know myself better.
- ☐ I hope to resolve difficulties with relationships.
- ☐ I want to change my career.
- ☐ I want to improve my health.
- ☐ I want to have a new perspective on an existing problem.
- ☐ I want to live an emotionally balanced life.
- ☐ I want to live a richer, deeper, more spiritual life.
- ☐ I want to blossom in my creativity.
- ☐ I want to understand situations that perplex me.
- ☐ I want to realize the purpose(s) of my life.

It is helpful if you consider a few of your goals, and keep them in mind as you decipher your dreams. Expect guidance and wisdom!

Dream Incubation

Dream incubation, an ancient custom used throughout the world, is used in order to come to a new awareness or solution to a problem in one's life or community. It is a practice that you can try at home with ease.

- Before going to bed, prepare your space so it is free from clutter and will heighten your senses.
- Prepare for bed with a calm mind and spirit. No TV!
- Make sure your dream journal is ready for recording. Write some thoughts in your journal about what might be troubling you.
- Come to a place where you have a clear, concise question regarding the situation.
- Write your question in your journal, as well as on a piece of paper to place under your pillow. The more direct the question, the more direct the answer will be. If you ask, "What am I going to do with the rest of my life?"

you probably will receive a vague answer. Be specific. "Do I want to accept the job that has been offered?" Be sure to write your question. I once skipped this step and awakened with a great dream (and possible answer), but couldn't remember what question I asked!

- As you go to sleep, be intentional about the question. Repeat the question over and over in your mind as you fall asleep. Allow images to come that relate to the question asked.
- If you wake in the night, be sure to note some of the dream images on your bedside dream pad. Incubation will not work if you don't record your dream. Incubation is not magic, although it is very effective.
- Upon waking in the morning, write all that you can remember about your dreams.
- Journal your thoughts about the incubated question.

If you commit the time to this incubation process, you will be rewarded.

Betty's Incubated Dream: Engagement
Emotions: curious, slightly anxious, accepting

Before I went to sleep I wrote an incubation question: "Should I commit to the Institute for Dream Studies (IDS) DreamSynergy™ Certification Program?"

In the early morning, I saw a brief but clear image of my hand with an engagement ring half way on my finger.

❧

With reflection, I realized that committing to the IDS program was about being able to really engage with myself. It was clear to me that the decision was up to me. Was I ready to wear the engagement ring? I needed to commit to the decision to focus on what I yearned to do!

Dream Recall

Below are some tips for remembering your dreams. You will also find your own techniques that work best for you to increase recall. Do what works for you!

Top Ten Tips for Remembering Your Dreams

1. Acquire a dream journal in order to manifest your intention to remember your dreams and your commitment to record them.
2. Get to bed a little earlier than usual. It is helpful to feel fully rested.
3. Avoid taking unnecessary medications before bed. Antihistamines and certain other medications can inhibit recall. Vitamin B6 and the herb Mugwort are thought to increase recall.
4. Before going to bed, put your recording materials (paper and pencil) by your bed and ask your unconscious to share a dream with you during the night.
5. Before sleep, open your journal to a new page, record the date and write a brief synopsis of your day.
6. If you wake in the night, focus on any dream images you have. Jot down a few words to jog your memory in the morning. Don't let your sleepiness talk you into believing that you will remember in the morning or that the images have no significance. It is easy to talk yourself out of the steps necessary for recall.
7. Some people find it helpful to drink extra water before bed so that they have to get up in the night, thus waking up just after a REM cycle and achieving recall.
8. Upon waking, resume the sleeping position you were in while dreaming usually your most comfortable sleeping position. This is a very successful tool. Try it!

9. If you have had no recall during the night and you cannot make any connections to your dreams upon waking, stay quietly in bed, eyes closed, and imagine some of the people in your life or some of the settings that are familiar to you. Sometimes just flipping through these images will stimulate a memory of a dream.

10. Write anything you remember—even if it is only one word, an emotion, or a physiological response. One word can sometimes lead you to important information. If you awake with a song or poem in mind, write it down. Nothing is insignificant. If you cannot remember anything, make a note to that effect in your journal. "I do not remember anything about my dreams last night." The process of writing often brings my dream back to memory. It's amazing how receptive your unconscious is to your true efforts.

REM (Rapid Eye Movement)

Most dreaming occurs during the stage of sleep characterized by rapid eye movements. In this period of sleep, the pulse rate quickens, breathing becomes irregular, and large muscles are limp. We are basically paralyzed during this period of sleep.

Wake Up! No longer can you fool yourself or others into thinking that you aren't dreaming! What are you waiting for?

CHAPTER 3

Be the Keeper of Your Dreams

We all dream; we do not understand our dreams, yet we act as if nothing strange goes on in our sleep minds, strange at least by comparison with the logical, purposeful doings of our minds when we are awake.
—Erich Fromm, *The Forgotten Language*

What if, so far, you don't remember your dreams? Don't worry. Use your waking life to start training your dreaming mind. Simply writing down an event in your life as if it were a dream can be very helpful in processing any stressful or unresolved event. Practice using the language of dreams with an occurrence in your life. Write the details of the event and describe the emotions you felt during the incident. Then process it as you would a dream. You will be amazed at the meaning that can be realized in this way. It helps us understand our waking life occurrences in a deeper way, with a larger perspective. Try it!

Justina's Waking Dream: Unhinged and Blinded

I have an accident as I am driving from Atlanta to Charlotte to visit my Mom on Mother's Day. Soon after getting on the interstate, I am shocked as the hood latch fails and the entire hood of my car suddenly flies up and wraps itself over my windshield, totally blinding me. I cannot see in the side view mirrors or in front of me. I have to trust and move over to the side with fast-moving traffic whizzing past me. I am filled with fear and panic. There is only a very small shoulder on the highway here in the midst of city traffic in Atlanta on I-85. I burst into tears as I call 911, but cannot tell them where I am since I cannot see out of my car to read any road signs. I climb over the seats and force my way out of the passenger door, although I can barely open it, for there is little room between the car and the concrete road barriers. I am terrorized as the cars whiz past me at fast speeds. It would be so easy for a car to slam into my car and then into me. I decide to climb over the concrete barrier into a busy exit area. I realize now that I am right in the midst of "Spaghetti Junction"—the busiest area of the interstate system surrounding Atlanta. When the police finally arrive, they make me get back in my car and I am feeling like no one really cares if I live or die. It is dangerous to get back in my car. Then AAA and the policeman tie my car hood down enough for me to peek through and they usher me with flashing lights to the next exit, where AAA can rescue my car. I am frightened beyond belief. I know it is a miracle that I have survived this accident.

☯

This episode affected me greatly. I was frozen with fear. It was all so beyond my control. I had recently moved to Charleston and did not have a lot of support. My body suffered greatly from the stress associated with the accident, and even Reiki and breathwork were unable to relieve the tension.

I decided to write out the incident and work with it as if it were a dream, which was very helpful.

In reflecting on the dream-like experience I wrote:

Traveling fast down major road of life, I am suddenly left with no vision of the road ahead. I need to slow down.

I need to look at what is blocking my vision.

I have to change my perspective.

"Blind Faith" —I am not in control. I have to trust that God will care for me.

We often call for help but it doesn't come when we think it will. Often seems so long, but it most often does eventually come—just not on our time schedule.

When I travel too fast, I become unhinged.

The hood covers and protects the engine and mechanics of the car. When I travel fast, I lose protection for my body.

Waiting is torturous sometimes.

"Hood" refers to community—motherhood, neighborhood. I am missing my "hood" since my move. I must create new communities.

Dream Recording

You already may be maintaining some sort of journal or diary, but I suggest that your dream journal be separate. Your dream journal is where you record your dreams, work through the dreams with exercises, and record the new understanding and lessons learned for your life.

Night Notes

To capture your dreams you will need to make some notes in the night. Dreams are like vapor for most of us and disappear the minute we wake up. So put your journal, or paper and a pencil, under your pillow or beside your bed. Or you might prefer a voice-activated tape recorder—unless you are sharing your bed with someone who objects to hearing your dream in the middle of the night.

The main thing is to jot down a few notes to pull you back into the dream when you wake up. It's easy to convince yourself in the night that you will remember the next morning, but don't believe it for a minute! Chances are you won't remember. Go ahead: make the commitment to your dream and write it down. You don't need to even open your eyes—just scribble a few words for a beginning.

One word can be enough to get you started!

I wrote this on my dream pad in the night:

We have a very strong floodgate with dreams—shuts quickly after dreamtime. The idea of the dream comes through— briefly—then access to dream is terminated.

Justina's Dream Series: Plowing the Fertile Field

These were offered to me only as images—one image per dream. There was no story line, no words, no characters and little emotion. The recurring dreams created a series that helped me be more patient with my progress.

1) August 8, 2011: Field of Dirt
   I see a flat field of dirt.

2) September 18, 2011 (month later): The Tractor Emerges
   I see a tractor rising out of a similar field. I can only see the front wheels, but know that it is emerging.

3) October 14, 2011 (month later): The Field is Furrowed and Ready for Planting
   I see a field of rich dark dirt that has been plowed and is ready to be seeded.

❧

These images came at a time when I was cutting back on my work commitments in order to have time in which to decide what my next endeavor would be.

I didn't think much about the image of the dirt field until I had the dream of the tractor emerging from a similar field. Then I knew I was on the right track (tractor) and making progress in finding fertile ground for my work.

When I had the dream of the plowed field, I was so excited! I knew that I was ready to sow my seeds for my next project! It reminded me again that to produce a successful yield, I needed to give time to the necessary preparatory steps. The visions encouraged me to move ahead in my work. In the dreams (visions), I realized that the progress was made without involving any conscious effort from the Dream Ego.

Many apps are available for recording dreams. Technology changes very fast, so I encourage you to search for them online.

I can only imagine what will be available in the future. Maybe we will be able to transfer the images of our dreams onto the screen. What a treat that would be! I am concerned, however, that some of the technology may hinder the mystery and magic of our dreams.

Remember that intention and commitment are primary prerequisites to successful dreamwork. Keeping this in mind, create a schedule for your morning routine that includes time for recording your dreams. Get up fifteen minutes earlier than usual and claim that time as a gift to yourself. You will be rewarded. What a great way to start the day—honoring your dreams instead of your deadlines. Try to open your mind upon awakening to your dreams; don't move into linear thinking about what needs to be accomplished today. Dreams don't really respect that type of thinking.

You are on your way when you begin recording your dreams. Once you get in the habit, it will be such an adventure. You are the writer, producer, director, set and costume designer, as well as all the actors. You will be astounded by your creative genius! Enjoy this process! It will change your life if you commit. Guaranteed!

You might want to print a copy of "Top Ten Tips for Remembering Your Dreams," and "Guidelines for Journaling Your Dreams" (printable versions of both lists are provided in the Appendices at the back of this book) and place them in your dream journal. I hope you already have your dream journal picked out and that it is ready to hold your treasures—perhaps you have been recording your dreams for years. Way to go!

Remember: You can't fool your unconscious. Dreams respond to Intention and Commitment!

Treat your dreams with the respect they deserve by creating a system for recording them. After all, you probably have some system for organizing your e-mail. Your dreams contain more important information for your life than your inbox does!

Dream Journals

You may not be in the habit of recording your dreams. You have your own style in all aspects of life, so honor your preference regarding what type of journal you use. Some people choose to collect their dreams in a beautiful journal, and others may type their dreams into a word processing document or dream journaling application on their computers.

In My Dream … a creative dream journal

Treat your dreams with the respect they deserve. I created a dream journal that guides you through the remember-and-record process. It has suggestions for working with your dreams, an index for your dreams, simple ideas for finding meaning, a vocabulary of emotions, and a recommended reading list. If interested, visit my website: www.DreamSynergy.org

Guidelines for Journaling Your Dreams

1. Keep paper and pencil by your bed. You may want to use a lighted pen or keep a small flashlight nearby. I write with my eyes closed in the dark. A pencil is dependable since it will write as long as it has a point, unlike a pen which requires being held in a certain way for the ink to flow.

2. Tape-recording your dreams is an option. Keep a sound-activated tape recorder by your bed. Make sure it is ready to record before going to bed.

3. When you waken slightly during the night, you may write a detailed account of the dream or just a few key words. Usually some key words will jog your memory in the morning. You will be rewarded by writing down as much of the dream in the night as you can recall. The way you phrase the dream in the night is often helpful in uncovering important information.

4. Upon waking, lie still with your eyes closed and review the night's dreams. Resume your favored sleeping position, which is probably also your favorite dreaming position. Once you enter linear thinking—for example, reviewing activities scheduled for the day ahead—your dream world is left behind. It is usually very difficult to retrieve dreams once you "hit the floor."

5. Immediately transfer your dream notes to your journal either by hand or on the computer. At this time fill in any details that are missing from your night notes. It is important to do this upon first waking because your dream experience fades quickly.

6. When recording your dream, write it in the present tense, as if it's happening right now. For example, "I am standing on a cliff watching a tidal wave approach." That makes it easier to re-enter the action, emotions, and energy of the dream.

7. Separate the dream text—or what actually happens in the dream—from your waking thoughts about what you dreamed. You can make connections to your waking life later, after you've recorded the dream.

8. You may want to include the following information in your dream journal. (Your personality will determine how you choose to record your dreams.)

- Write the date and your location.
- Write the narrative of the dream story, with as much detail as possible. Describe the characters, setting, conversations, incidents, colors, and emotions.
- Do not make personal connections to your life at this point—write only the dream story.
- Create a title for your dream. Don't get caught up in giving a title. Just jot down the first thing that comes to mind. It will provide an easy handle for use in the future.
- Identify the basic emotions of the dream. How did you feel in the dream?
- Describe any physiological symptoms you experienced as you recorded your dream; for example, "My stomach cramped," "I felt nauseated." Note the part of the dream you were recording when you experienced these symptoms.
- If you did not write a synopsis of the previous day's activities on the previous night, add one now. This will be very helpful later when you go back to work a dream. (Add this information *after* you have recorded the dream so it doesn't interfere with your recall.)
- Draw sketches of any parts of your dream. Drawings help you understand the meaning of your dreams and take you back into the dream easily.
- Immediately note associations that come to you. Leave space to work in more depth on your dream at a later time.
- Make an index in the back of your journal. For each dream, list the date, title and basic emotions.

Wake Up! ... to your daytime life as well as your dream life. Please don't ignore these gifts of the night. What are the important messages to your true self?

CHAPTER 4

🌀🌀

Learn the Metaphorical Language of Dreams and Life

The unconscious aspect of any event is revealed to us in dreams, where it appears not as a rational thought but as a symbolic image.

—Carl Jung

People ask, "If dreams are so important, then why aren't they presented in a way that is easy to understand? If they contain significant messages for us, why aren't the words not simple and to the point?"

Why?! Because we would probably turn a deaf ear as if it were extraneous noise; and therefore it wouldn't open the message so personally and universally to each individual.

Words are limiting. Dreams come from a source that is beyond words, from the expansive and evocative world of images, metaphors, and symbols. It's true that "A picture's worth a thousand words." You can write a thesis about one picture. In viewing a picture, you project your personal experience into the images and create meaning for yourself. In the same way, dreams open you up in a way that allows you to connect to emotions and to both personal and universal meanings.

A young child can repeat words that adults say, but he can't use them in a meaningful way until he really understands what the words mean. On the other hand, at a very young age a child learns to interpret the situations and images around him; he learns to communicate not with words but by sending and understanding visual cues: reaching, pointing, or using facial expressions. It is helpful to think in this way when working with your dreams.

Like rabbis in ancient times, Jesus used simple stories, called parables, to help people understand his teachings. He used characters and images taken from everyday life to illustrate His message through symbolic stories. The parables offer wisdom for the ages, for all people, in many situations. So it is with dreams. The symbolic meaning is powerful and expressive; it is timeless, relating to our past, our present and our future. We cannot pin down one meaning of a parable or a dream. They are always open to further interpretation.

The definition of a parable is very similar to a description of dreams: a short story or mini-drama that uses images and familiar situations to teach a moral lesson, religious principal, or universal truth. The parable uses what is known to illustrate something that may be unknown.

A parable might use an analogy, such as "the kingdom of God ... is like a mustard seed ... or like yeast" (Luke 13:19, 21).

Think of the following parable as you would a dream. What is the metaphorical language? What is the message that is being shared? How does the story have personal significance in your life?

Scripture: Luke 15:3-7

3 So he told them this parable: 4 "What man of you, having a hundred sheep, if he has lost one of them, does not leave the ninety-nine in the wilderness, and goes after the one which is lost, until he finds it? 5 And when he has found it, he lays it on his shoulders, rejoicing. 6 And when he comes home, he calls together his friends and his neighbors, saying to them, "Rejoice with me, for I have found my sheep which was lost." 7 Just so, I tell you, there will be more joy in heaven over one sinner who repents than over ninety-nine righteous persons who need no repentance.

> ⌇
>
> In this parable a shepherd leaves his flock of ninety-nine and risks his life to find one lost sheep. Although we may have never even seen a flock of sheep and certainly not tended a flock, the parable can be interpreted to help the listener or reader understand God's concern for his children who go astray.

You may not realize that you are already familiar with symbolic and metaphoric language, but you use it every day of your life. Think of the symbols that we all recognize and to which we respond. These symbols are extensive in their meaning.

As we drive, we are guided constantly by symbols on road signs; they direct us and warn us, and even change our behavior. A railroad crossing sign is not static; it always means, "A train might be coming soon"; but it also warns you to slow down, stop, look, and listen. The sign also may bring up memories of trains from your childhood, or remind you of a tragic accident you witnessed. And signs that use symbols are potentially universal in their ability to communicate—even someone who does not speak the country's language can understand what the sign means. No matter in what country we travel, we can follow road signs through symbolic language. Arrows show us the way, and crossed lines tell us to be alert as we approach an intersection.

A heart—no words, just an image—represents love, heart health. A stylized image of a man and a woman tells us where to find the toilet. No words are needed. This is symbolic language.

From the time we learn to count, we use symbols to represent quantity. A "2" is not a word, but it is a symbol that has both personal and universal significance; "2" represents mathematical value throughout the world, no matter the language, but it also contains your personal associations and memories. What does "2" mean to you? It is a mathematical number, and also connotes a pair, balance, duality, a couple. What was happening in your life at the age of two?

In mathematics we use signs like +, =, %. What do those mean? It's hard to define fully, because the symbol broadens the meaning. For example, the + ("plus sign") might encourage you to contemplate the notion of *addition*—perhaps adding something to your life—but the symbol also has metaphoric significance as a cross, suggesting something spiritual, or perhaps a crossroads. The addition, subtraction, division and multiplication signs indicate specific functions—the way in which we are to manipulate the values presented in the "problem." How might we add, subtract, multiply or divide something in our lives in order to solve a problem?

You may have a favorite t-shirt that is so worn out that others think it's nothing more than a rag. But to you, it has value beyond words. You cherish it because it reminds you of something special and meaningful. For you it is much more than just a t-shirt; it is a symbol of a special occasion, an accomplishment, friends, or a place you visited. It might have so much meaning that you could write an entire book about all the memories and experiences it represents and the feelings it elicits. The t-shirt maintains a universal meaning, as well; it is a garment worn in casual or sport settings throughout the world.

People want me to interpret their dreams, but I respond that I don't interpret other's dreams. Unless you use your personal experience and insight, you will not discover the personal messages your dreams hold for you. If I assume that I can tell you what your dreams mean, I would be fooling not only you, but also myself. My interpretation would have more to do with my life than your life.

Universal and Personal Symbols

In your daily life, you encounter many objects and experiences, and respond to them in both personal and universal ways. For example, as a universal symbol, the ocean may represent the vast unconscious, deep emotions, freedom and/or expansiveness. But because you have personal experiences and associations to the ocean, it also can be a personal symbol rich with meaning that is specific to you. For example, if you have had a frightening experience and are uncomfortable in water, the ocean's meaning for you will be very different compared to its meaning for a surfer or a scuba diver.

Although we each have our individual associations to symbols and characters, we also share similar associations to certain images throughout many cultures. Some symbols carry universal meaning around the world. This is especially apparent when I work with dream groups of members from various countries. Although the culture and language are different, the essence of the symbol is similar.

Carl Jung refers to universal and archetypal symbols that carry similar significance to all people. He attributes these phenomena to what he called the "collective unconscious."

Knowledge about which you are unaware, which emerges in a dream, may be attributed to the collective unconscious. If an ancient symbol or archetypal character appears in a dream, research it to learn more. It's remarkable how much you know, but are unaware that you know!

Carl Gustav Jung (1875 -1961)

A Swiss psychiatrist who founded analytical psychology. He created and developed the concepts of archetypes, extraversion and introversion, individuation, the collective unconscious, and synchronicity. Jung's work has influenced psychiatry, religion, philosophy, anthropology, art, and literature.

Waking Symbolic Language

Even with no words accompanying them, these symbols elicit messages.

What does each of these symbols represent to you? Practice using symbolic language in your daily life.

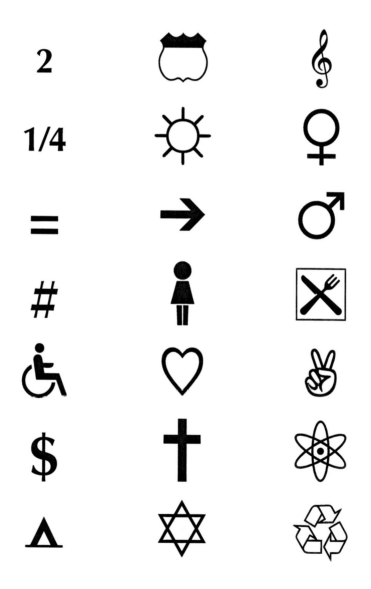

Exercise: Dialogue with the Unconscious

This exercise uses "active imagination" to generate a dialogue between the dreamer and his unconscious. (Active imagination is described at length in Robert Johnson's book, *Inner Work*.)

The dreamer chooses a character from a dream and assumes that character's point of view. (Note: It is important that the dreamer select a dream character who is *not* part of his waking life. It is surprisingly easy for the dreamer to believe after the exercise that the friend, spouse, or parent actually said and felt the things that come up in the active imagination. If the dreamer is emphatic about wanting to use a dream character who is someone he knows, instruct him to refer to the character using a generic term— for example, "the angry man," "the jealous friend." It is important for the dreamer to keep in mind that the character represents a part of his own personality, not the waking-life acquaintance, friend or relative.)

ॐ

Throughout this exercise, keep your eyes partially closed; this helps you stay in the role of the character in the dream.

1. Close your eyes and imagine that you are in your dream observing the setting, the colors, the emotions, and the characters of the dream.

2. Wait for a character to appear. It might not be the character you would consciously choose. The character who appears may have a seemingly small role in the dream—perhaps even an observer with no active role.

3. Invite the character to come talk to you.

4. Allow the character to answer the following questions. Record the answers (using your non-dominant hand) in your journal.

"Who are you?"

"What should I call you?"

"Why are you here in the dream?"

"What do you want from me?"

"What do you know that I don't?"

"What is the most important thing you have to tell me?"

Reflections from Tzivia

One night during a recent visit with my mother (who is suffering from age-related memory loss), I went to sleep feeling sad, small, angry, and frightened over what is happening to her. This is the woman I have known all my life as a smart, cultured, loving, and generous being. And now she has trouble remembering the names of her closest friends, how to calculate a tip, and what errand she left the apartment to run.

That night I dreamed that I was telling a friend "Nothing matters." There wasn't much more to the dream than that.

I woke feeling oddly reassured, but also confused. Could the dream's message be true? "Nothing matters," sounded nihilistic and hopeless in the light of day.

I brought the dream snippet to Justina. "It's just a little dream," I explained, almost apologetically, before we began our dreamwork.

Tzivia's Dream: Nothing Matters (Or Everything Does!)

Emotions: accepting, concerned, unsure

I'm telling someone that nothing matters. Nothing matters in her life.

It doesn't matter if she writes a book, whether she changes or saves lives in her writing, nothing matters.

But as I'm saying it I wonder if it's true. She could argue against all of it. I say if she didn't write the book, someone else would.

Nothing matters. But things do matter. Her books do matter. I go back and forth in my mind. I don't know if I'm being cruel or wise.

But she's looking at me as if she's also not sure about what she's saying, but she is willing to be convinced.

꩜

Justina led me in an exercise in which we engaged in a dialogue with the dream. Justina asked questions and I responded in the voice of, and from the perspective of, "Nothing Matters."

Here is an edited transcription of that conversation between Tzivia (in regular font) and the voice of Nothing Matters (in italic font):

Where do you reside? *High in the clouds.*
What are you? *I'm a lighter view.*
What is your purpose? *To hold everything.*
Why? *To help it make sense.*
To whom? *Individuals.*
Why do you care? *I love them. They are burdened.*
Why? *Because they are attached to all that happens. They're on a roller coaster with ups and downs.*
How can you unburden them? *I remind them it doesn't matter.*
Why would people do anything if nothing matters? *They do things anyway. They have to do them more lightly, with less attachment.*
Does it have to do with enjoyment rather than purpose? *The enjoyment should be higher.*
How do people get to understand and not resist? *When things start coming apart—then they see it. When you see it from a high perspective, what looks like coming apart on the ground, looks like a pattern of flowing, unified movement. It's neither good, nor bad. It just is.*
What is your worst enemy? *People being blind. Not seeing me.*
What causes them to be blind? *They are so individual and separate. They cling and hang on.*
What are they hanging onto? *Meaning. Their own self-importance. The ego.*
What does matter? *Connection, the big picture. What they can't see.*
How can they understand it? *They need to trust it and feel it.*

How would you teach that? *By bringing them up here with me so they can see for themselves. It's a helpful, loving view. It would help them tolerate things. I'd tell them to think back and forward as far as they can. Play with perspective.*

But I'm losing my mother. I feel devastated, angry. It feels like the end of the world! *Nothing is lost. You are always loved. You are part of everything and so is she. Just breathe, relax, and trust. I know it is hard to do that without a mother.*

Where do I find my strength? *It's inside.*

I feel empty. *Close your eyes and let go. Little by little you will understand.*

I need to come to your perspective. *I will find you in your dreams and bring you up here so you can see.*

～

That was the end of the dialogue, and the end of my dreamwork session. When Justina and I finished, I just sat, stunned in the silence. This wise dream voice, coming through me while I was awake, helped me find the perspective I needed to cope with my mother's new reality, and my new relationship with her, now that her cognitive abilities are in decline.

I share this story and the dialogue with others because I believe this dream and its message are not meant for me alone.

It is a difficult balance to achieve. Realizing that what matters to us most in the world is indeed precious and beautiful and wholly indispensible and at the same time, all that really matters are the things that are invisible, formless, and timeless. This dream dialogue has helped me see the situation from this perspective, and as much as possible to remember the big picture when I start to slip into worry and sadness.

For example, it really doesn't matter whether or not my mother can remember the name of her favorite restaurant or the plot of the movie we saw together the day before, but her love for me and mine for her: that truly does matter.

Archetypes

The insight offered by an archetypal dream is unending. Because archetypes are transpersonal, they offer us a perspective on a bigger universe. It is beyond our individual concerns. We are pulled into the history of human existence.

Jung identified certain dream symbols that possess the same universal meaning for all humans. Your personal experiences and dream experiences often touch on universal themes and symbols. These symbols are believed to occur in every culture throughout the history of the world.

Major Archetypal Characters

Jung identified seven major archetypal characters:

1. **The Persona**: Your representation to the world in your waking life. It is the mask you wear in public. In dreams, the persona may or may not resemble you physically or as you behave. The persona can appear in your dream as yourself or as another character.

Self

Webster's definition of self (pertaining to our ego-self) is "the identity, character, or essential qualities of any person or thing." Carl Jung introduced the word Self (using a capital S to denote the difference from the ego-self) to refer to a "supra-ordinate, inner, unknown, divine center of the psyche which we have to explore all our lifetime."

I believe that one's true nature—that is, the authentic Self—is the person that one is born to be: in other words, one's God-given nature. It is not influenced by outside factors. I will use this idea as a working definition for the role of self in the process of change.

Removing My Mask

Many years ago, when I studied at Pacifica in Santa Barbara, California, I had a memorable experience with my Persona Mask. One of the activities assigned involved making a gauze-maché mask. There were no guidelines other than instructions and guidance on how to create the mask on my face so that it actually took on my personal facial features. From there on we were free to go in any direction. Most people created fanciful and beautiful masks. I wanted to create a beautiful mask, but my inner child wanted a mask that depicted what I had worn all my life. I was surprised how the mask evolved without planning. I painted it with rosy cheeks and pink lips. It looked happy and nice, but I connected pieces of wire to the mask that created a cage-like appearance when I put on the mask. I connected the wires with brads so that it could not be taken off and on.

I realized that this was my Persona Mask that I had been taught and expected to wear at all times—happy, pleasing, nice, looking good! I decided that I was ready to let go of this unauthentic mask that I presented in public. My dreamwork had prepared me to take it off and reveal my true authentic Self that had been afraid to come out for so long. That true Justina had made everyone in my family of origin uncomfortable, and I had often been punished for being myself or expressing emotions other than happiness.

No words can describe the terror I felt as the night approached for us to present—one by one—our masks and the story behind them to the large group. I could not believe how terrified I was. I told my classmate (and new friend) that I could more easily get up and take my clothes off in front of everyone than remove my Persona Mask. It is hard to believe now the fear of revealing my true Self. I stood up with my mask and wires attached to my head, told parts of my story and carefully removed my mask. I cried and shook with terror.

The next day a friend and I went to the nearby shore and ceremoniously destroyed the mask, sending safe parts out to sea; and other parts I buried deep in the sandy cliff nearby. I will never forget the power of that ritual and experience. It has supported and encouraged me to never wear that false mask again, but instead to let my divine light and authentic emotions be visible to others.

2. **The Shadow**: Your rejected and repressed aspects. The shadow

is the unacknowledged side of your personality. It contains a group of characteristics which our egos regard as unacceptable or inferior—you believe these parts are "not like me." Generally you do not recognize that you possess the qualities that you assign to the shadow, which resides in your unconscious. However, you can easily see those qualities in others, and often project your own shadow characteristics onto other people.

In dreams, the shadow may be represented by characters such as a bandit, a pursuer, or a boss. Often the shadow is represented by an unknown character that makes you mad, sad, or afraid. It is important to learn to accept your shadow qualities in the individuation process.

> **Individuation**
>
> A term used by Carl Jung to describe the personal process of moving toward wholeness and completion, or to the true "Self." It is a process of integrating various parts of yourself (ego, conscious, and unconscious), becoming closer to your authentic being and the person you were born to be. Through individuation, human beings are formed and differentiated from other human beings.

The shadow also includes positive attributes. Carl Jung referred to unacknowledged positive characteristics as the "golden shadow." These are aspects of the Self which we project onto others (for example, in hero worship). We do not recognize that we have precisely the same quality that we admire in the person onto whom we are projecting, but usually that trait is part of our own genuine nature, as well.

It is in discovering and owning our shadows that we begin to find balance in our lives.

After a couple of years of working with dreams, I felt deeply that I was getting ready to do some major personal inner work, but I didn't know what it would be. Then I had the following dream:

Justina's Dream: My Hidden Shadow
Emotions: ok, curious

I walk into my backyard. I notice on the ground the outline of a person. It is a darker shade than the grass. I wonder who or what it is.

ॐ

As I described the image to my dream group, I said, "It was actually like a shadow." I was amazed that I had not been able to see that analogy until I expressed it aloud. I was getting ready to look at my "Shadow"—major work for sure! And, of course, I had it hidden in the backyard! In our dreams, we often put things in the backyard that we want to hide from public view.

3. **The Wise Old Man/Woman**: Often represented by a teacher, priest, shaman, nun, pope, medicine man, monk, Indian chief, or other person you consider to be your mentor. These characters appear in your dreams to guide you, offering words of wisdom.

4. **The Divine Child**: A representation of your innocence, vulnerability, and defenselessness. It also symbolizes your aspirations and full potential—"the seed that was planted at your making." The Divine Child often is represented by a baby or young child.

> *Give me a candle of the Spirit, O God, as I go down into the deep of my own being.*
> *Show me the hidden things. Take me down to the spring of my life, and tell me my nature and my name.*
> *Give me freedom to grow so that I may become my true self— the fulfillment of the seed which You planted in me at my making.*
> *Out of the deep I cry unto thee, O God.*
> —George Appleton

5. **The Great Mother**: Your nurturing or caregiver aspects, she may appear in your dreams as your mother, grandmother, or other nurturing figure. She provides you with love and positive support. In contrast, "Negative Mother" energy may be depicted as a witch or hag representing seduction, guilt, or control.

On one of our annual visits to New Hampshire, we visited the top of Wildcat Mountain. The Appalachian Trail crosses at this point, and I was drawn to two young women sitting at a picnic table, obviously off the trail for lunch and a rest. I began a conversation with them and found that as a graduation present to themselves, they committed to hiking the entire Appalachian Trail from Georgia to Maine. It had been a rough past three months for them and they could actually see "home" from that view, but had several more weeks to go. They were determined to finish what they had begun. Of course, I asked them if they remembered any of their dreams. They laughed out loud. "She has had really weird dreams," one of the young women exclaimed about the other. I asked her to please share with me.

Basically, in her recent dreams she had a beard that grew longer and bushier along the last parts of the trail. That is all she needed to say—I smiled as well. She thought she dreamed of the beard just because most of the people they encountered on the trail were male and had beards.

I suggested that she might want to congratulate herself on calling forth and embracing the "animus." That aspect of her personality allowed her to do the tough work of the hike that she set out to do. It involved setting a goal, undergoing great adversity, accepting challenges, and finding the strength to complete the goal. Yes, emotions (of the anima) might just turn us around, away from such undertakings, if not balanced with the animus. It was obvious the anima had not been lost; in addition to resting, the young women were creating woven bracelets out of strands of colorful embroidery floss to help fund their adventure. (Of course, we bought several!)

6. **The Anima/Animus**: Jung referred to these as archetypes of the soul. Animus encompasses traits that are "masculine"—that is, more outward-directed and concerned with going out into the world and doing. Anima embraces personality aspects that are "feminine"—more inner-directed and concerned with being comfortable with emotions, people, and creative energy.

   Everyone possesses both animus and anima, but generally speaking we are not conscious of them. It is helpful in your journey to wholeness to balance these aspects of your personality. As you begin to embrace these aspects of yourself, you may find yourself in the dream with a beard or dressed in women's clothing.

Justina's Dream: Nurturing my Animus
Emotions: tender, loving, remorseful

I'm carrying my little baby boy. I look at him with new eyes and think how I have neglected loving him enough. I think, "I've never really seen him as adorable as he is." I kiss him dearly on the cheek. I encourage him to kiss me. I want him to feel really loved. I've neglected him far too long.

ॐ

My "nurturing mother" part is finally recognizing the attractiveness of my animus. I am finally giving love and attention to my masculine side—the part that is capable of taking the lead in developing a balanced personality for me. I know this part is necessary to be successful in graduate school and my work. I am aware that I am beyond childbearing age, but I can still enjoy the tender relationship with my animus. I had not recognized before how attractive ("adorable") this kind of energy is and regret that I have not been more attentive to this masculine energy earlier in my life.

7. **The Trickster**: Your inner joker. Like many dreams, the Trickster plays jokes and provides humor to keep you from taking yourself too seriously. This character often makes you feel self-conscious or embarrassed by making fun of you or exposing you.

Archetypal dreams often are referred to as "mythic dreams," "great dreams" or "big dreams." They usually occur at transitional periods in your life, often leaving you with a sense of awe and empowerment. They are often extremely vivid and stay in your mind long after you experience the dream. Do you remember an archetypal dream?

A great resource for learning more about these symbols of the collective unconscious is Carl Jung's *Man and His Symbols*.

Collective Unconscious

Collective unconscious is the term Carl Jung used to refer to primordial images, experiences, and feelings that are part of the human psyche. This part of our unconscious is a deep pattern that flows through all of humanity throughout the world.

Justina's Dream: Alligator Brings Terror to Family Reunion
Emotions: anxious, afraid

I'm at a family reunion. From an upstairs area, I look through a glass window down toward a big indoor swimming pool. I notice a large pipe that empties water into the pool from the outside. I imagine how it would be if a whale came into the pool with the water that had recently poured in from lots of rain.

Suddenly I spy an alligator in the pool. I am horrified that someone may jump in and not know it is there, so I run down the stairs quickly. After I notify someone, I don't get involved in the situation. It seems like everyone else is involved. I'm aware that I could be the "hero" but I am not interested. I go into the pool area and notice people working to catch the alligator. They have lowered a red iron cage in the water and are trying to get the alligator to swim into it. Inside the cage is another cage with a man inside, as bait for the alligator. There are some other people in another part of the cage. I am not sure what their role is. The alligator finally swims into the cage. When he sees "human bait" he gets very excited and begins to thrash about, trying to get the man. He vigorously shakes the cage with unbelievable strength, increasing the force as he continues his attempt to reach the man. I am very scared and extremely nervous that the alligator will tear the cage and man apart. I am so afraid I will see the water turn red with blood. The entire pool quakes with force and I am overcome with fear.

⟳

How appropriate that the dream opens at a family reunion. I am there with all the parts of my family generations, past and present—all the characteristics and qualities that make me who I am today. I am looking through a window at an indoor pool below; the view provides a new perspective about what is happening—safely, behind a protective glass.

Rainwater from the outside is being fed into the pool through a large pipe. "Rain" is an archetypal image that often represents spiritual messages and blessings. It's being channeled inside, which relates to my opening myself to considerable spiritual insight in the previous weeks, instigated by a dream conference. "Rain" is necessary for growth and is appropriate as an image of the pouring in of new experiences in my life. As an archetypal image, the "pool" is the container of the unconscious—a symbol of the Self.

At first I muse about the possibility of a whale coming through the pipe with the rainwater. It seems to feel like an unlikely event, but not a threatening idea. The "Whale" represents the archetype of the "Great Mother," non-threatening aspects of nurturance and femininity. The whale also represents "huge amounts of spiritual food for thought." It is interesting how our psyches trick us into facing shadow figures! First it presents me with an acceptable and safe image (the Whale), but then changes it into its shadow image of the Alligator (Shape Shifter?).

The "alligator" is an archetypal image of the "Devouring Mother." It leads me into the shadowy world of instinct—the vicious passions of life. It is at this point that fear enters the dream. I must immediately do something to warn all the parts of myself that may enter the realm of the unconscious.

Was I going into dangerous waters? The image of the Devouring Mother brought up many questions for me. Considering part of its meaning as a representation of my biological mother, I ask myself whether I still fear her wrath if I let go of the traditional role of wife and mother that she modeled for me. As a representation of my own instinctual and aggressive nature, the alligator may be alerting me that I am going to have to tangle with the dangers of opening myself to these shadow parts.

How did I appear to my family (more important, how did I appear to myself) as I continued on my personal journey? Is the power of opening myself to my true nature frightening? Does it need to be feared? Will this bring chaos into my life? Am I going to be eaten up by leaving the traditional roles I have played?

Alligators live in the swamp. I know that I have entered the "swamp" in my life journey. It's part of the unconscious that I have never explored—seeming murky and dangerous. I do not know where to step next—dark and inhabited by unfamiliar things. It is so fitting to bring the Alligator, a swamp animal, into my dreams.

It is interesting to me that I no longer want to be the "Hero." As an archetype, the Hero represents the "Savior" and undergoes trials of strength, most frequently alone. Often the Hero is betrayed and killed or sacrificed.

It was true. I no longer wanted to play this role in my life. I didn't want to be the Savior of my family—neither my family of origin nor my present family. I wanted to take a healthier role. I was willing to be responsible, but I no longer wanted to rescue everyone from his/her inadequacies.

As I look at the image of the "man" placed inside the cage, I relate it to the "animus" archetype; this is the part of me that honors my potentials, thinks clearly, makes decisions easily, and manifests my creativity in the outer world. The animus is playing the role of the "Sacrifice." Have I sacrificed my animus in the past to appease or contain the Devouring Mother? Is this part of a martyr complex? Is it worth the sacrifice that I make? I was beginning to understand my role as a human sacrifice.

The masculine figure is put in a cage inside of another cage to protect it from the alligator. Have I put myself in a cage in the past? The cage in the dream is strong and red. The color "Red" represents raw energy, force, aggression, power, courage, life force and passion. How much energy does it require to keep this part of me safe from outside forces of nature? Do I feel trapped or "caged" in my traditional role?

In the dream, my ego stands on the sidelines, in total fear of what is happening. I watch as the forces of nature shake the container I have used as protection. I have never witnessed such dangerous power! I am frightened beyond description. I realize the terror of my Soul! With tremendous anxiety, I wait for the appearance of blood. The loss of blood often symbolizes death. Is the fear so great because I fear my own death? Does it seem as if I will die if I try to face the power of the Devouring Mother or the Swamp Animals?

The dream abruptly shuts off as I am dreaming—the images have been turned off. Was the anxiety too great to face? Was it too painful to confront? I look at the dream now and realize that the alligator never got to the man in the cage; he did not die. The alligator's power and fury were potent, but ultimately not destructive. I can face such vicious shadows and live! The fear was real, but the result for my life was certainly worth the risk.

Your Personal Dream Dictionary

Create your personal dream dictionary in a separate journal (or as a document on your computer) so that you can continue to use it alongside all the dream journals that you fill. You may want to create your personal dream dictionary in a spreadsheet on the computer, or a loose-leaf notebook or address book may be convenient so that you can alphabetize your symbols. Use whatever works for you.

In your personal dream dictionary, record recurring symbols from your dreams, and include the following:

- Symbols and all of your personal associations to each one
- Characters, plus three adjectives that describe each character
- Settings
- Colors
- Numbers
- Animals

After you write your personal associations, explore ancient and archetypal symbols for additional ideas. Add the ones that resonate with you. This is *your* dream dictionary.

My Personal Dream Dictionary

Art: Creative aspects that I nurture and often those that I do not nurture. Often an encouragement to play with my creative muse and spend more time in those endeavors.

Atlanta: Adult life, family-/community-oriented, pain of divorce, good friends

Bea: Caretaker, kind, always there when I need comfort and nurturance

Beach: A place of relaxation, fun, renewal, friendship

Christmas: Family and friends, celebration, Christianity, customs, gifts, deep loss of family, creativity

Corinne: Creative, spontaneous, adventuresome, thoughtful

Dogs: Fear from being bitten as a child, devoted to master, obedient

Family Reunion: All that contributes to my being who I am. The generations that help develop my beliefs, values, preferences. Helps me see the different aspects of myself represented by various people in my family. Sometimes seems to represent my past, present and future through the different ages of family members.

Foreign: Unknown to me, positive new experiences, adventure

Girl Scouts: Accomplishments, leadership, skills, fun, responsibility, out of doors, camping, friends

Horse: Fear, accident, power, lack of control, uncomfortable

101: Address of my childhood home

3: Number of children in my family, both as a child and as a parent

Purple: Favorite color from the time I was a child, unique, feminine, expresses me!

Silver Satellite: My first car, independence, college, generous gift

School: Success, respect, enjoyment of learning, good times, vulnerabilities

Woods: Childhood, freedom, adventure, at one with nature

Common Dream Symbols

Many symbols are common to dreams. Learning more about some of these symbols may help you better understand the dream's language. Don't try to memorize or learn what others have recognized as the meaning for the particular symbol, but reach within and realize what the symbol means to you.

Bridge: This symbol often represents a connection, transition between two parts of your life, or an important change. How you are crossing the bridge and the emotions expressed in the process may give you clues to what supports you or sabotages you in your transition. Is there a transition going on in your life? The type of bridge and what it crosses may offer additional meaning. Is it a footbridge, large bridge, modern, old? Does it cross water, a deep gorge, a highway or railroad track? How are we making the journey across the bridge? By foot, car, bus? Is the bridge a familiar bridge that holds memories for you, or is this untraveled, unfamiliar territory? How do you feel about crossing the bridge?

Mary's Dream: In a Rut
Emotions: anxious, aware

I am traveling in a car across a narrow bridge. As I come near the middle of the bridge I realize that I can go no further. I get out and survey the situation. My wheels are caught in a rut in the roadbed. I must get help, I cannot continue the journey on my own.

❧

One of the students of Institute for Dream Studies (IDS) had this dream before she began the program. She realized that she had started her personal journey and individuation process, but that she kept getting caught in the "ruts" of her life, preventing her from getting to the new territory she yearned to reach. She decided at that time that she needed help to continue her personal journey and committed to the IDS program. What "ruts" prevent you from crossing the bridges in your life?

Snake: Often appearing in dreams, snakes have the universal meaning of change and transformation. The snake is the only animal that sheds it skin as it grows. They are used in some spiritual rituals as a symbol of wisdom, mysticism, and the energetic forces of the *kundalini* (the life force that resides at the base of the spine—dormant until awakened, as in yoga). Snakes also are depicted in the Rod of Asclepius that represents health and well-being. Our personal relationship to snakes offers additional meaning. Are you afraid of snakes, or do you respect snakes in their habitat? What is the posture of the snake? Is it in attack mode or minding its own business, slithering away, or guiding you? How do you feel about the snake?

Wallet: Often lost, stolen, or found in dreams. What does your wallet represent? What would someone know about you if she found your wallet? Probably lots about your identity and sense of values—your name, where you live, what types of and how much money you have. And a woman's purse offers even more about the owner; just think of all the clues to your personal life that are contained in a purse. If you've lost a wallet or purse in your dream, ask yourself whether you have lost or are beginning to lose a sense of who you are. Perhaps you find a wallet that has been misplaced for quite some time. Are you reclaiming your authentic being after losing it in the past? If so, way to go!

Fence: Often represents boundaries, limitations, and blocks to further advancement. The fence might hinder you or it might protect you from negative influences. What type of fence is it—what is your personal association to that type of fence? How do you feel about the fence?

Recipe: Look carefully to see if a dream recipe might represent instructions, guidance, or a solution; also be alert to the possibility of it being "a recipe for disaster."

Justina's Dream: Don't Fence Me In
Emotions: concerned, afraid

I am in my backyard. I need to move outside of my yard, but a chain link fence is blocking me. It is too tall to go over and is attached firmly to the ground so I cannot go under it. I feel stuck and fearful that my way is blocked.

〇〜〇

Years ago, I shared this memorable dream with one of my dream groups. A member asked me to close my eyes and see if there was any opening that would allow me to pass beyond the fence. As soon as I closed my eyes and imagined the scene, I broke into laughter. I saw that the fence was only about four feet wide, and did not connect to anything on either side. I had focused so much on the "obstacle" that I missed the wider view and opportunities to move outside of my limited boundaries. What a lesson for me! It still reminds me to look with a more expansive view when facing obstacles.

Dream Settings

Dream settings can provide many clues. Since our dreams do not necessarily represent time and space as we know and live with them, settings are often difficult to understand. How can it be that in your dream you are in your childhood home and also in a building where you now work, or even in another part of the world—all at the same time? Remember: Dreams don't care about our notions of time and space.

The setting in the beginning of the dream often shows you when a particular issue began in your life. Perhaps the issue you are facing now as an adult is rooted in your childhood. Comparing the past circumstances with the present may help you realize something that will help transform the challenge for you.

Is your dream setting in a city or in the country? How do you feel in the dream in that setting? What are your connections to that setting in your waking life? Do you need more quiet reflective time, away from the busy-ness of city life?

It's important to list recurring settings in your personal dream dictionary. Below are a few possibilities to consider. (Remember to honor your own personal meanings above anyone else's suggestions. You may have a reaction that is very different from the possible associations listed below! It's your dream you want to understand, so make sure you listen to your thoughts and emotions about the setting.)

Day: Easier to see clearly, open, waking life

Night: Difficult to see clearly, frightening, unknown, mystery, ability to see moon and stars, death, rest

Country: Pastoral, quiet, nature, restorative, less sophisticated, remote, isolated

City: Busy, action, work, community, opportunity, social, adventure

Foreign Land: Unknown, a different culture, memories of a particular experience, somewhere I've never been before, adventure

Shore: Broad perspective, close to body of water, restorative, playful, nature, at the edge of the unconscious, transition

Mountains: Spiritual, high perspective, challenge, higher realm of consciousness, pinnacle, rugged terrain

Home: Familiarity, security or danger, shelter, comfortable, basic needs; pay attention to when you lived in that home

High School: Adolescence, peer pressure, fun, learning, challenging transformation, anxiety, accomplishments, process of maturation, freedom

Colors

Color amplifies your dream's meaning. I am amazed at how the universal quality of a color ramps up the dream message. Because color relates to emotion at the deepest unconscious and physiological levels, it is best *not* to ask what the color *reminds you of.* It is always best when working with color to ask, "How does the color make me *feel?*"

One of the first colors that people report in dreams is red. How do you feel when you visualize red? Red universally represents blood, life force, anger, emergency, love, and/or passion. Do you like to wear red? Look at personal and universal qualities and think of your dream in those terms. Does that give you additional information about the personal message of your dream?

Remember your personal dream dictionary. Add a list of colors that appear in your dreams. Write your personal associations to those colors. Check out Robert Hoss's book *Dream Language: Self-Understanding through Imagery and Color* for excellent information about working with the colors in your dreams. In your dictionary, add additional comments about how the colors resonate with you.

Just to get you started:

Red: Intense emotions, passion, anger, love, sex, emergency, life force, vitality, injury, stop

Black: Darkness, the unconscious, shadow self, death, mystery, masculinity, fear, authority, power

White: Spiritual, purity, innocence, new beginnings, truth, sterility, unpainted canvas, clean

Blue: Tranquility, emotions (water), heavenly realm (sky), spiritual, truth, wisdom, loyalty, hope, contentment

Yellow: Cowardice, happy, intuition, optimistic, well-being, caution, the sun (warmth), spontaneity, vitality

Brown: Grounded, family, belonging, comfort, earthy, physical, reliable, solid, practical

Purple: Romantic, feminine, intuitive, philosophical or magical, royalty, imagination, spirit, creativity

Grey: Void of emotion, sober, practical, pragmatic, compromise, inability to see clearly (fog), gloomy

Green: Growth, nature, healing, rest, balance, calm, renewal, serenity, prosperity (money), envy

Gold: Enlightenment, the sun, the divine, wisdom, masculine, generosity, the higher self, preciousness, spiritual gifts, talents

Silver: Moon, femininity, intuition, tranquility, precious, valuable alloy in alchemy

Pastel colors: When a pastel color appears in your dream, think of it in terms of an undeveloped version of the primary color. If you dream of pink, perhaps you are just beginning to embrace your passion.

Dreaming in Black & White

Some people say that they only dream in black and white. Even some "dream experts" say that many people do not dream in color. My belief is that we all dream in color (including black and white), but some people are more aware of color in their dreams than others, just as some people are more aware of color in their waking lives.

When people have told me that they dream only in black and white, when we do dreamwork together I make a point of asking questions such as, "What color are the trees? What color is the sky? What color are the houses?" They answer without hesitation, "Oh, the leaves on the trees were green" or "The sky was a soft blue" or "One house was red brick and the other brown shingles."

Often after I hear a dream in which little or no emotion is expressed, I ask what colors are in the dream. The dreamer frequently responds, "Actually it was all grey." Of course! Grey often represents a subduing of emotional energy. We may say, "It's a grey day." Life loses color when we don't honestly experience our emotions. Or perhaps we are beginning to move out of a black and white (wrong vs. right) way of thinking and accepting some new grey areas in our life. Perhaps we are more open to other ways of thinking, less judgmental. That would be a good thing!

Begin to look for color in your dreams and your frequent recognition of color will follow—both in your dreams and in your life.

Numbers

Numbers constantly amaze me. How can we know? Even though you might not be consciously aware of what a particular number represents universally or culturally, your psyche seems to know. As with other symbols, there are several ways of looking at numbers to amplify your understanding of a dream on both the universal and personal levels.

Jung considered *three* to be a mystical number, representing mind, body, and spirit. In spiritual traditions, it is often a holy number; for example, to Christians, it may represent the Trinity—Father, Son, and Holy Spirit. The number three frequently occurs in fairy tales (Three Little Pigs, Goldilocks and the Three Bears), and some magical traditions include such practices as "turn around three times," "clap three times," "knock three times," etc.

More specifically, what are your personal associations with three? What happened in your life at the age of three? Were you one of three siblings? What was Third Grade like for you? Relate these thoughts to a particular dream that incorporates the number three. Add these thoughts to your Personal Dream Dictionary!

Here are some "starter ideas" for considering the meaning of numbers in your dreams:

One (1): Unity, circle, the Self, the best (we're #1), beginning

Two (2): Duality, opposites, balance, subconscious, yin yang, "tension of the opposites"

Three (3): Trinity, creativity, mind-body-spirit, triangle, "three's a crowd"

Four (4): Wholeness, four elements, square, honesty ("he is fair and square"), four seasons, four phases of the moon

Five (5): Five senses, five digits of hand, adventure, change

Tension of the Opposites

Jung taught that if the tension between two opposing forces can be held independently without yielding to the urge to identify with one or the other, then a third unexpected force may emerge which will unite the opposing forces in a new, creative way. Try it—sometimes it's very hard to hold on without moving to one side or the other, but it's worth the wait and tension to embrace the new way of being.

Justina's Dream: Success and Misfortune
Emotions: ok, concerned, glad, empathetic

A friend has a successful store. I am with her at some point and she mentions that something happened. (A fire or break-in?) I find that it occurred at a second store that I wasn't even aware she had. I congratulate her on her success with her business and offer condolences on the unfortunate occurrence.

❧

In reflecting on the dream the next morning, I wrote the question, "When is success followed or accompanied by misfortune?" The written answer was immediate: "Always! It's life's rhythm. Good news/Bad News, Progress/Setback, Joy/Sorrow, Success/Failure. The good news is that it's cyclical: Good News, Bad News, Good News, and so on!"

I couldn't believe that new understanding came so quickly and felt so comforting when thinking about upsets in life. I wrote, "Don't get caught in the negative!" as my lesson for that day—await the positive!

Modes of Movement

Think of all the types of movement or transportation we experience in both waking life and dreams. Have you ever considered how they are alike, and how they are different from one another—metaphorically and symbolically? You can probably understand this symbolism on your own, but let me get you started.

There is a major difference between riding on a bike and riding on a train, in both waking life and in your dreams. Riding a bike requires balance and your own exertion, and you are exposed to the elements. You are more susceptible to personal injury on a bike, but you can blaze your own trail. You don't have to follow the tracks that a train follows. You don't have to go along with the crowd. You can go places where other forms of transportation cannot go. You are the one determining your course. Maybe riding a bike reminds you of freedom in your childhood.

On the other hand, a train follows not only a route determined by others (track), but also follows a schedule. You have to yield to a route and a timetable that are not your own in order to get to your destination. You have to invest in a ticket—no free ride! You are part of a community of fellow travelers and you can sit back and relax. Maybe the dream is letting you know that you are "right on track" with your journey or you are "being trained."

Other questions regarding movement in a dream are: Why am I changing location? How does that make me feel? Am I using the wisest form of transportation to reach my destination?

Now, what are your personal associations with bikes and trains? Write them in your dream dictionary!

Traveling in a car might signify traveling alone or with a small group of people. You still need to follow a road to get to your destination, but you have control over what route you take and what your schedule will be. You can even choose what kind of car you travel in and what color! Does that car remind you of one you have owned or driven in the past? When? How does that amplify the meaning of your dream?

If you are in the back seat, you have little control over where you are going. Is your ego giving over the responsibility or control to someone else, or to another part of yourself? Do you need to get in the driver's seat or is it about time you got in the back seat and let someone else do the driving for a while?

This dream came to me after I started letting go of excessive control in my life.

Justina's Dream: Taking a Back Seat
Emotions: ok, comfortable, happy

I get into the back seat of a car. A friend is driving the car and another friend is sitting in the front passenger seat. I am very comfortable being in the back seat and enjoy just going along for the ride. It is a great new feeling of not carrying the responsibility for the group.

◌◌

For once, I was not the responsible one making the decisions, leading the way, blazing the trail. It was definitely time for me to let others take some of that responsibility—or another part of me, maybe a more fun, flexible part of Justina. I used that dream as a reminder to let others take the leadership role and for me to enjoy the ride.

Animals

 Animals often appear in people's dreams, playing many roles and carrying lots of energy and symbolism. Sometimes they are personified in a dream, acting like humans.

How do species differ from one another and how are they the same? How might a dream animal represent aspects of you, acting and reacting in various ways?

A dog is obedient, loyal, dependent, and attaches itself to a master, whereas a cat is tough to train, independent, a hunter. Dogs and cats are alike in that they are both instinctive, and most of the ones we encounter are domesticated. In what way might the cat or dog represent aspects of your personality? What can you—as a cat or dog—learn about your relationship with others?

You may be surprised how perfectly a particular animal represents a waking life situation, making it possible for you to more clearly see your own behavior by comparing it to that of a dream character (in this case, an animal).

Let's look at a few additional animals which appear frequently in dreams:

Bear: Power, motherly love, fierce protection, hibernation

Bee: Stinging, buzzing, busy, creator of sweetness

Bird: Wisdom and intelligence, joy, goodness, hope, aspiration

Bull: Vital energy, obstinacy, strength, power, assertiveness

Horse: Power, freedom, sexual energy, femininity, speed

If an animal appears in your dream, list your associations in your Personal Dream Dictionary. You also might want to learn about the characteristics of a particular animal by reading Ted Andrews' *Animal Speak: The Spiritual & Magical Powers of Creatures Great & Small.*

Marge's Dream: Heroic Hamster

After having occasional dreams in which she has forgotten and neglected, or carelessly treated, caged hamsters, causing her to feel sad and guilty, Marge had a very different kind of hamster dream. It revealed that she had definitely turned a corner. At the time she had this dream, Marge was transforming her life after a divorce by returning to college and working toward a BFA degree.

Emotions: anxious, afraid, amazed

A brown brick house in the country is on fire. I watch as a large, brown hamster escapes through a window. The hamster is leading a mouse and shows it the way out of the burning building. The hamster is a hero. It is big, strong, intelligent, compassionate, knowing, and able!

ꙅꙅ

This is a huge change from the sickly caged hamsters in my earlier dreams.

Hamsters are a regularly occurring personal dream image/character. One of my first pets was a hamster, and I have had quite a few other hamsters as pets. I accept it as my totem animal.

The brown in the dream represents a need for grounding and stability in my life, which I was claiming. I was also claiming my ability to succeed and be my own hero.

I (the heroic hamster) am now leading my own timid self (mouse) out of the structures that confined me in the past.

Metaphors

Dreams represent actions, situations, events and characters through the use of metaphor. A metaphor is an image or symbol that represents a larger concept. It can be interpreted in a variety of ways, thus expanding the possibilities for meaning in your dreams.
Some examples of metaphors you might find in your dreams are:

Broken heart: Your heart is not actually broken, but it feels like it has been torn apart by a loss or disappointment. The dream may depict a heart as broken into pieces and that image might help you better understand how you have been affected emotionally.

Hold your horses: The dream may have a scenario of you being asked to hold on to some horses, but may be actually suggesting you slow down a bit and be more patient in your response to a situation.

Rollercoaster: If you are experiencing many ups and downs in your life, your dream may include the image of a rollercoaster.

Crossroads: Do you arrive at a crossroad in your dream, unsure of which way to turn? How does that relate to your current life situation? Do you need to make a choice between one thing and another?

Snake in the grass: You may actually see a snake in the grass in your dream. Is there a situation in your life where you need to be cautious of a person who is sneaky and untrustworthy?

Break the ice: In waking life, have you used the term "ice breaker" to describe how people get to know each other at a large gathering? In your dream, is there a suggestion that might "break the block (of ice)" or in some other way help to make a difficult situation more comfortable?

Ellie's Dream: Underwater

The day before my move, I was finalizing paperwork for selling my house the next day.

Emotions: afraid, relieved, comfortable, peaceful

I am in a beach house with my husband and my sister-in-law. There is flooding and the water is quickly rising into the second story. We are sitting on a mattress and although I am fearful, I am aware that my sister-in-law is not anxious or worried. We then proceed to float out a window on the mattress and drift on the floodwaters until we eventually wash up on dry ground on a quiet street corner. We stand up and begin to walk around, feeling free and grateful to have so easily avoided the crisis.

~&#127;&#127;~

Initially, I was frightened by the rising water, but then we were magically lifted to safety without much effort of our own. There was a sense of calm.

My sister-in-law is generally at peace and not usually ruffled by circumstances—a happy, thankful person. In this dream she brought me peace, helping me to call on the part of myself more like her that could release my anxiety over selling my home, which financially was "underwater!" (Aren't dreams amazing? I didn't realize the connection of being "underwater" until it was brought to my attention.)

The mattress certainly represented another source of stress for me surrounding the move. My sister wanted me to give her one of the beds in my house; I felt misunderstood and taken advantage of by her at the time. In the dream the mattress floated easily to safety, avoiding the crisis. In waking life, with my husband's support, I was able to let go of the anxiety surrounding her demands and all worked out peacefully.

I felt peace and relief after this dream and, as in other dreams, I realized that everything always seems to work out if I can let go of my anxiety and trust that all will eventually be well.

Homonyms

Dreams often contain a word that sounds like another word (bee/be, olive/I love, eye/I) that also fits the situation. We are so creative in our sleep! Often it is not until you read the dream aloud to someone that these "puns" are discovered.

One of the first dreams I shared in a dream group included the statement, "I took my shoes to the shoe store. My sole needed repair." Of course, I only thought of it as a shoe sole, but with the insight of the group, I opened up to the message that my soul needed repair. It brought tears to my eyes. I knew at that moment that I was on a quest to take care of my own soul.

Homonyms are more often heard by others listening to your dreams. Focusing on the literal scenario in your dream sometimes makes it more difficult to hear the play on words.

Practice by saying aloud these phrases. How might you hear them differently?

- I wished to create an attractive bow but knew that I did not have the right approach. (bow/beau)
- My fans were yelling boos from the grandstands. (boos/booze; Are you drinking too much?)
- I went to the dealership. I was told that I needed brakes (breaks) in order to protect myself. (brakes/breaks)
- Someone had left cents on the table for anyone to take, but I was too preoccupied to take advantage of the offering. (cents/sense)
- I am amazed that my heel is illuminated by elevating it. (heel/heal; Was this the key to my healing—a spiritual path?)

- In pure exhaustion, she turned in to a hostel. (hostel/hostile; A hostile position?)
- If the doctor could only attend to his patients. (patients/patience)
- I was unhappy and walked out on a pier to reflect on my life. (pier/peer; Do I need to disconnect from my peers in order to find myself?)
- I knelt to pray on my success. (pray/prey; Am I taking advantage of others as I move up the corporate ladder?)
- I found my journal and began to write the conversation that I had with my spouse. (write/right)

Connie's Dream: The Nazis are After Me
Emotions: anxious, afraid, relieved

The Nazis are coming. They have their searchlights out and are looking for me. I am running through a big open space, trying to find a place to hide. I try this and that—but there isn't a safe place. Finally, I find a secret door that goes through the wall into a French café. It feels like I am in a movie. I wait here with other people to plan what we will do next.

૭৲৩

I had this dream after I had been diagnosed with cancer. Nothing felt real. My life seemed like a screenplay. I was able to ask myself "What am I not seeing (Nazi ing)?" What rigid, rules-based part of me was trying to have power and control over my diagnosis and treatment? The notion of finding "cover" in a French café reminds me of the French Resistance during WWII; was I offering resistance to disease or resistance to giving in to disease while facing cancer treatment? It was comforting to know that I could find solace with others in a French café, a place to enjoy the camaraderie of friends.

Dream Themes

Water

Water is the source of life and carries broad universal meanings, as well as personal meanings. Emotions often are represented by water. But what type of water?

River, Ocean, Pond, Puddle, Rain, or Snow? Each has its own traits. Is the water (emotion) flowing, frozen, murky or dammed up? The depth and expansiveness of the unconscious often are represented by the ocean, whereas a puddle may represent the beginning of expressing emotions. Our interaction with the water in the dream often shows where we are in our journey to open up to the unconscious. Are you on shore, on a pier, in a boat, or actually floating on the surface or diving deep into the ocean?

Pursuit, Chase

Running from something, pursuit of something, fear of being caught, insecurity. Who is chasing you or whom are you chasing? Are they really chasing you or just trying to keep up with you? Confront them and find out what they want from you. Maybe they have a message or even a gift to give you.

Flying

Freedom, elevated, new perspectives, lightness, escape. I remember flying dreams from my youth and have always loved the feel of flying. But you may feel differently about flying in a dream. It may be frightening. We have to let go of control in order to fly. We are not grounded, but we do have a great perspective.

Justina's Dream: Learning to Let Go and Fly
Emotions: anxious, afraid, delighted, joyful

I am flying around some interior rooms and am very hesitant about it—sort of holding back out of fear.

Then I decide to let go and really enjoy it. I hold my arms out in front of me and really go fast and enjoy it. It is such fun when I let go.

കൂ

This was a short snippet within a longer dream, but oh, so powerful! It was a reminder that when I let go of control, I enjoy life more and feel less anxiety. I use the great feeling of exhilaration in the dream to remind me in my waking life that I have more fun when I let go of trying to be in control of situations and myself. This relieves stress immensely.

Brian Andreas's *Story People* contains the following quote: "If you hold on to the handle ... it's easier to maintain the illusion of control. But it's more fun if you just let the wind carry you."

Death

Transformation, opportunity for a new beginning, letting go—not a warning of physical death! It seems like death would not be a good event in a dream, but often it is just what you need! Is there an aspect of your life that prevents you from succeeding in living the life you want? Is it time to let that part of yourself or that belief system die?

Justina's Dream: Dying and Burning Home and Property
Emotions: accepting, focused, slightly concerned

I plan to die and create a plan and prepare. I am not afraid or sad—it's just the way it is.

I will also burn down our house, destroying all—nothing of that property will be left behind. I am methodical in all the plans. Our property slopes down to the shore—water and beach. I have taken out a few things to save. Some dolls, etc.

I start the burn of the house. Some things burn easily but some things have a fire retardant and won't burn.

I have longer to die than I thought I would have. I am not concerned, but I don't want to frighten people who think I am dead so I stay out of sight for the time being.

I know some people close to me are beginning to realize that I am not dead yet.

ॐ

I knew by the lack of emotion in the dream that it was about letting go of a part of myself rather than about physical death. What part of me was I ready to let go? Perhaps the part that no longer wanted to be identified solely by my role as homemaker. With the death of the part of me that answered always to family and friends, I would be free to choose which roles I wanted to live out in my life. Letting go of a role that I played successfully throughout my adult life was difficult—it didn't happen as quickly as I imagined. Setting fire to my house (in the dream) began a transformation process. And not everything related to that role in my life burned; some things seemed to be resistant to the burn. Interesting that I save my dolls—they have always been supportive of the authentic Justina. Water and beach would be left—ahhhh. The Charleston I love!

Birth

New beginnings, creativity, personal change. Are you pregnant in the dream? You may be gestating a project or an idea, and/or be at the beginning of a new, creative time. How far along are you in your dream?

Justina's Dream: Can't Hurry the Gestation Process
Emotions: excited, disappointed

I know I am pregnant and am excited about my arriving baby. I think that I am ready for delivery but look in a long mirror and see that I am only slightly "showing." Wow, I really thought it was time for delivery! I realize that I am only in my first trimester. I know that this will take some patience on my part.

❦

After the graduation of a class of my Institute for Dream Studies (IDS), I took a sabbatical to decide where I wanted to head in the next step of my work with dreams. I knew that I needed to step back and allow myself time for rest and reflection. I was pushing myself to know my answer. I asked myself, "Why don't I know what I am going to do next?" After writing my dream down the next morning, I began to make connections to my waking life. "Oh, my! It's not time for the new birth of my next project. I am only in my first trimester of gestation." I then realized that it had been two and a half months since graduation and became more patient with the process of delivering my new "baby."

Nudity

Open, exposed, vulnerable. How do you feel being nude in the dream? Are you embarrassed, or concerned about how it might make others feel? Or are you unconcerned and enjoying the freedom and authenticity of being uncovered? There is often a progression in a dreamer's "nudity dreams," marked by embarrassment in early dreams, and eventually evolving to a lack of concern or even feeling comfortable about being nude ("revealed, exposed") in later dreams.

Justina's Dream: Nudity Series (Over a three-year period)

1992: I'm at a party and realize that I don't have on a skirt or pants. I am terribly embarrassed and grab a towel to put around me. I feel like everyone else is staring at me and making fun of my exposed body.

At this point, I was still uncomfortable allowing others to see me authentically—still tied to appearances, wearing masks, and afraid to show my vulnerabilities.

1998: I am in the midst of friends. All of my clothes are see-through. No one else seems to notice. I don't know why I wore this outfit. What was I thinking? I am very uncomfortable but attempt to go on as if I am not exposed.

I had begun to shed my masks, still a bit tentative. I was starting to realize that others were not judging me as much as I was judging myself.

2002: I am at a public gathering. I am having a great time with everyone and am not concerned about my clothing—or lack of clothes! I do not have on a blouse—only a very short skirt. It does not feel inappropriate in any way.

I was surprised when I recorded my dream that I felt so comfortable being exposed. I realized that I was actually at ease now with exposing my vulnerabilities, shadow sides, and authenticity.

School (Exams)

 Preparedness, being tested, grades. When you take on a large project or challenging presentation, you might dream of having to take an exam and realize that you have not been to class or even read the text. And then you can't even find the classroom! Have you had these scary dreams? Bet you have! Don't worry. You are just reminding yourself to prepare ahead of time for the projects at hand. These dreams also reveal how much anxiety you are feeling; recognizing this may help you stop and focus on what needs to be done to feel better prepared.

Justina's Dream: History Exam
Emotions: anxious, upset, nervous, somewhat relieved, afraid

A friend and I go to take our next exam—mine is a History exam.

I am anxious about the exam. I want to do well. I finally get to the classroom. I've made a concise study sheet with dates and other information, but can't find it in my book bag. I keep searching with no success in finding the study sheet.

I am nervous. I ask a guy friend a couple of questions, dates, etc. He helps some.

I can remember so little. I want to make a good grade so it won't pull down my grade point average. (The setting/mood/feeling reminds me of my Junior High School.)

ↄ৲ↄ

In waking life, I had been preparing for my mom's ninetieth birthday party. I was carrying lots of anxiety about pleasing my parents and meeting my father's expectations, as well as about being the hostess for extended family. My family "history" brought up lots of anxiety about doing it well enough to please them. Junior High always represents a time when I felt especially vulnerable socially and uncomfortable with myself.

The dream made me aware of how much anxiety I was carrying, and I stopped and tried to relieve some of that by asking for more involvement from other members of the family. In my journaling, I found ways to reduce my own expectations of myself.

Sexual Encounters

Intimacy, creativity, merging, acceptance, self-love. People often are concerned about dreams in which they are having sex with an old flame or the next-door neighbor. These dreams rarely have anything to do with a desire to connect with that person in waking life. By identifying the characteristics of the sexual partner in the dream, you can identify a part of yourself that you would like to reconnect with—maybe an undeveloped aspect or one long forgotten. Try asking yourself, "What are three characteristics of the character in the dream?" Sexual encounters in dreams could also bring up instances of vulnerability for you, depending on your past experiences.

In one of my workshops, Joe told about his recurring dreams of having affairs with a former girlfriend. He was continuously bothered by this. He felt happily married and was anxious when dreaming of the affairs. He shared his anxiety with his wife, trying to be open and let her know that he was not interested in his former girlfriend. Because neither of them understood that dreams are directly related to our own personal characteristics rather than expressing a desire for another person, tension grew between them. The dream character actually became a wedge in their marriage relationship.

It took only a few minutes of discussion with Joe for his anxiety to turn into relief and excitement. When he understood that this dream character (former girlfriend) might represent a part of him, he began to cry. Really! The recurring dreams had created a strain on his whole being and marriage— thinking that he might unconsciously want something outside his marriage.

He realized that he actually *did* want something. He wanted to claim his Anima—his creative, feminine energy—which had been represented in his dreams by his former girlfriend! She was in art school when they dated, and he had spent his life in the corporate world and did not allow time for his inner "artist." He clearly understood for the first time that he yearned for his creativity to take a priority in his life.

So much of his life became clear in a period of ten minutes. It was a memorable time for me, as well, to witness once again how quickly the dream leads us to where we need to go to live more authentically and joyfully.

Thinking like an Apple (or Trusting like a Child)

When we got our first computer for the family back in the 1980s, I constantly asked, "How does it work? Why does it do that?" and exclaimed, "That is impossible!" It was all out of my comfort zone. My narrow perspective prevented me from reaping the rewards of our computer; I wanted to know how it worked before I would use it.

Our daughter, aged three, approached it with a "Wow!" She crawled up in the chair, fully believing it was her new toy (tool) and that she could use it—and she did! No hesitation, no questioning.

A friend's son, Nathan, who was in the Fifth Grade at the time, drew a picture of the workings of a computer as part of a contest. (He won the national contest, by the way!) His drawing depicted hundreds of little people inside the computer running the programs; this was the way I was used to seeing things happen. Nathan's drawing spoke my language and matched my perspective of how to complete a task.

Later, a computer tech told me, "If I teach you one thing, I want you to not ask why. … The computer can work without your interference or understanding exactly what has happened." (Actually, I still resist and ask why—but not nearly as much.)

I resisted learning, trusting, and benefiting from this new computer technology. In a similar way, many people resist exploring their dreams, because dreams use a different language that many believe is too complicated to understand, even for their own benefit.

You already know that acquiring skills to use your computer benefits you; so it is with dreams!

Weddings

New beginnings, change, merging, commitment, love, balance of male/female energy. Dream weddings bring together two aspects of the dreamer's personality, honors and ritualizes the union, tradition, sacredness, and commitment, union of the anima and animus (Jungian terms for the feminine and masculine principals). In the individuation process, the dreamer will begin to see those aspects uniting within the self.

If you are actually planning a wedding in waking life, you may have nightmares about weddings. They may be offered to us as an example of how catastrophic it could be, which makes us so happy when nothing so appalling happens at our wedding! Explore all of the scenarios as both waking-life fears and as metaphors.

@/@

Wake Up! ... and enjoy the themes of your dreams! Are you becoming more fluent in the language of dreams? You will probably begin to look at life and conversations metaphorically. It's fun and rewarding!

Chapter 5

◎◎

DreamSynergy:
Dreams + Action = Change

A dream is the mirror of the soul, bringing us a clear view of ourselves and the learning situations in which we are involved ... showing us aspects of ourselves we hadn't noticed, letting us see the roles we are playing, and revealing how we think we appear as opposed to how we really are. ... All of these incidents give us important insights about our lifestyles which help us to understand ourselves better and to make our lives more complete and satisfying.

—Wilda B. Tanner

My philosophy of dreamwork, which I coined DreamSynergy™ (DS), is an eclectic combination of beliefs, experience, and knowledge that allows you to become greater than the sum of your parts (your life experiences, current situations, relationships, and your dreams themselves). Through my work in the field of dreams I have developed exercises and processes that allow you to move toward your authentic Self, by yourself, by focusing on three specific aspects of a dream: emotions, characters, and beliefs. This is done not only by understanding each of these things, but also by taking the action necessary to recognize and bring that knowledge into your waking life.

Thus, Dreams + Action = Change! Like anything else, you must be willing to put the effort into understanding the dream to take advantage and reap the rewards. Within dreamwork you can choose to operate at three different levels and each level will allow you to delve deeper into resurrecting the "you" you are born to be. Those levels I call: Recap, Relationship, and Recognition. These will be discussed later in this chapter.

Through the DreamSynergy™ (DS) method of dreamwork, you will learn to uncover the message of your nighttime dreams and use that message to help change your life and move closer to your true nature and unlimited potential. Throughout this dreamwork, the sacred nature of the dream and the dreamer are honored, as well as the authority of the dreamer in determining the meaning of the dream.

The flexibility of DreamSynergy™ allows the dream to lead the way with practical step-by-step applications that are easy to use by individuals, dream therapists, or in a group process. The dynamic approach of DreamSynergy™ revolves around the concept that Dreams + Action = Change, creating personal growth and transformation through commitment to the process of change.

The emotional, mental, and physical healing that occurs in the process supports you in dealing with the challenges of relationships, career, finances, and health. The process encourages you to keep the dream alive in order to continue to gain new meaning and understanding.

DreamSynergy's three key components:
- **Emotions**
- **Characters**
- **Beliefs**

DreamSynergy's three levels of dreamwork:
- **Recap**
- **Relationship**
- **Recognition**

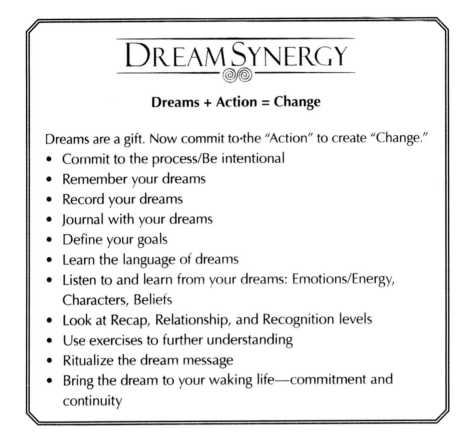

DREAM SYNERGY

Dreams + Action = Change

Dreams are a gift. Now commit to the "Action" to create "Change."

- Commit to the process/Be intentional
- Remember your dreams
- Record your dreams
- Journal with your dreams
- Define your goals
- Learn the language of dreams
- Listen to and learn from your dreams: Emotions/Energy, Characters, Beliefs
- Look at Recap, Relationship, and Recognition levels
- Use exercises to further understanding
- Ritualize the dream message
- Bring the dream to your waking life—commitment and continuity

Focus on Emotions

Examining the emotions you feel—both within the dream and upon waking—is a powerful key for unlocking the dream's healing message. These dream emotions are related to your waking-life emotions. Working with them helps you to recognize feelings, reactions, and denial that you may be experiencing in waking life.

Emotions lead to feelings, which lead to thoughts, which then lead to actions. (It is important to process the emotion before it leads to an action.) Emotions affect every aspect of your life.

Investigating the causes of emotions in dreams will help you begin to understand the causes of your waking-life emotional actions, reactions, and decisions.

Dreamers frequently are surprised by the intensity of emotions in a dream. The action or situation in the dream may not seem to warrant such strong feelings. You will gain deep insight if you pay attention and ask, "When do I feel a similar emotion in my life?" The waking emotion will probably not carry as much intensity because you have learned to camouflage it in order to ignore it.

Unexpressed Emotions

In waking life you may have learned to conceal your emotions from others, and perhaps even from yourself. Over time, unexpressed emotions have a tremendous impact on your health, relationships, choices, activities, and attitudes.

You are only fooling yourself if you believe that you are protecting your relationships by not expressing your true feelings. You cannot successfully hide what you feel! It will eventually be expressed—if not frankly and honestly, then disguised in another form, often one that is damaging to you and your relationships—as passive-aggressive behavior, aggression, or other manifestations.

By becoming conscious of the emotion, you can choose to change negative, damaging behavior by managing your reaction. When you gain an understanding about what causes that emotion, you can begin the process of defusing the cause so that eventually your emotional response is not so strong. Understanding makes it easier to choose when and how to act on the emotion and its circumstances.

Justina's Dream: Terrorized That I Might Be Stung
Emotions: Afraid

Wasps are everywhere in my home. Honey is dripping down the walls.

Everywhere I go, I see the wasps. I am so frightened that I am going to be stung. I don't know what to do.

I'm really upset. I don't know how to avoid being stung and how I'll get the wasps out of my home. (Bad taste in mouth as I write this in my journal. I feel like I might throw up.)

I don't know how to get rid of the honey. It needs to be dissolved so I can get it off the walls. I don't know what dissolves honey.

I know it's up to me to take care of the wasps. I can't expect anyone to help me. It's my responsibility.

I am so frightened of being stung! No one else seems to be frightened of the wasps.

I knew as soon as I woke up feeling fear and anxiety, that it was the sting that I feared, and that this dream was about my relationship with the man I was dating. I had not realized that my anxiety was so great that it was making me sick (nauseous), but I recognized that it was true. I had been masking the great fear and anxiety that I was feeling about "being stung."

So much of our relationship was like honey—sweet, but I knew that I was about to be hurt. The sting of a wasp is a very painful sting. It hurts so much! I was sad for myself that I was carrying around that much fear.

I began to seriously look at the stickiness of the relationship and wondered if it needed to be dissolved. I wondered why I had wasps with the honey although in waking life I knew that honeybees are the insects that produce honey. By quickly researching the difference between wasps and honeybees, I found that wasps are more aggressive predators and are capable of stinging multiple times.

It was interesting that no one else in the dream was afraid of the wasps. The wasps were not after them, but were directed at me. The dream made it very clear that I was the one who was going to have to protect myself by taking action.

It was soon after that I dissolved the relationship, realizing that I no longer wanted to live with the sting and hurt.

Bringing Emotions to Consciousness

The dream brings our emotional state to consciousness. Please pay close attention to all the feelings associated with your dreams—the emotions within the dreams and those you feel upon waking. Make note of emotions when recording your dreams. Characters in a dream may express or represent different emotional states. Pay attention!

It is surprising how many people cannot identify what emotions they are feeling. Can you? If you are a person who has a particularly difficult time identifying and working with emotions, you will probably find this the most powerful dreamwork you do. By understanding and naming your emotions, you will begin to see how they affect your life.

In daily life, some people deal with painful emotions by quickly dismissing them and covering them up with activities such as eating, smoking, exercising, drinking, or working and staying busy. They try to subdue the emotion so they don't feel the pain. The damage this can do to your body, mind, spirit, and overall well-being is enormous.

Carolyn's Dream: Asleep on a Frozen Shore
Emotions: full of dread, terrified, numb, resigned (AFRAID), determined, confident (GLAD)

It's late evening; calm and peaceful weather. I'm on a rocky, icy mound next to a frozen ocean. Behind me the snow- and ice-covered hill rises. I fall asleep. I awake. It's dusk, almost night. Everything seems foggy and grey. The tide has risen and sloshes against my mound. I realize I'm in trouble.

I inch my way backwards, reach my foot into an icy, slushy puddle. To my left are small rises – also icy slosh leading to high ground. I must get there. I'm surprised that I'm not chilled through. I inch forward slowly, knowing that if I slip into one of the pools, I'll

---

surely freeze. There's no one around to hear me if I scream or call for help. I can see high ground. I'm determined to get there, to reach and endure old and jagged rocks and risk getting wet.

❧

The week before this dream, my mind was cacophonous; I went for a Reiki treatment. During the session, I felt a whoosh of energy, became shaky, felt every emotion in a raw state. During the ensuing week skies were bluer, marshes more lustrous, bird songs and ocean waves louder. My heart tumbled in a racing bubbling river, expressing itself in torrents of joyful tears. At the same time, I was more afraid than I ever remember being.

Five days later, I had this dream. I saw the contrasts between how I'd been living, and what more there could be. The path wouldn't be easy—I had almost seventy years of encrustation to shed. I felt how much I'd cut off my emotional body from just about everything—how much fear I'd been holding onto and not expressing. I buried myself in an endless list of things to do. I thought I was through grieving my husband's death, but I'd been living in loneliness and resignation, annoyed at interruptions from the safe harbor of solitude. Perhaps most of all, how I'd been thinking, "Maybe I'm not good enough for what I wanted."

I began to pay attention to how I was feeling at any given moment with the aid of the "Vocabulary of Emotions" chart. I knew that I was going to have to allow myself to let the ice melt and that would cause me to feel the pain of my loss. I enlisted my acupuncturist to help me let go of the physical pain created by holding on to my emotions. I am developing mantras to train myself to believe that I'm a truly wonderful person. I pay more attention to the dreams instructing me to play with color, dance, and music. I am now more mindful, heartfelt. I have deliberately set forth to create a path of joyful living. After two months, it's getting easier every day.

Basic Emotions

Emotions are especially interesting because of the power they hold for those who are making major changes in life. Over the past two decades, I have thought, talked, read, and dreamed about emotions and developed the Vocabulary of Emotions chart (see page 96) to help you more easily identify your emotions.

The Vocabulary of Emotions chart lists words that my dream group members have used in the past to express emotions. By no means does the list contain every word that expresses feelings, but it is a helpful tool in identifying basic emotions. Find a word that describes the feeling in your dream, and then refer to the column heading to identify the basic emotion.

I believe that our basic and true emotions are those we are born with. They are not what we learn from parents and society, but instead are part of our authentic nature. Imagine a newborn baby. What does a baby feel? All of its actions and reactions can be categorized as GLAD, SAD, MAD, or AFRAID. These four basic emotions are the headings for the chart. It is important to understand that any particular emotion is neither more nor less positive or negative than the others. They all contain both positive and negative energies. The positive or negative charge comes from how the emotion is expressed— appropriately or inappropriately.

Perhaps you are afraid that you will lose your job. You may have been taught that you "should" never be afraid. Why shouldn't you fear losing your job if you know that the company is downsizing and you have already watched colleagues losing their jobs? Don't hide the fear, but instead ask yourself "What am I afraid of?" and then "What can I realistically do to protect myself?"

One of the most challenging areas of dreamwork is how people talk about emotions. It would be ideal if everyone expressed emotions in basic, non-ambiguous language, but when I ask dreamers about the emotions in a dream, the two most frequent words they use are "confused" and "frustrated." These words are used to camouflage the basic emotions; both "confused" and "frustrated" are easier to acknowledge than "afraid" or "mad." It is more socially acceptable to say "I'm frustrated with you" than "I'm mad at you!" People feel less vulnerable saying "I'm confused" than saying "I'm afraid."

Until you can identify the basic overall emotion, it is difficult to know what action to take. What does one do in "confusion?" Usually confusion leads to more confusion, which leads to even more confusion, putting you in a cycle of uncertainty. It is difficult to move beyond the bewilderment. By contrast, if you name the emotion as "fear," you have more opportunity to make positive changes. You will then be able to ask, "What am I afraid of, why am I afraid, and what can I do to overcome the fear?"

The same is true with "frustration." Frustration usually leads to more frustration and again you stay in a cycle of disturbance. If instead you name the emotion in a more accurate way, you may find you are "mad." Now you can ask. "Who am I mad at? What am I mad about? What am I going to do about it?" That will give you much more useful information in order to proceed and act in beneficial ways.

A dreamer stuck in "confusion" and "frustration" is in a circular pattern, going nowhere; but when he owns the words "mad" and "afraid," he can move forward on a path of personal growth.

Positive and Negative Qualities of Emotions

As pointed out earlier in this chapter, emotions are not intrinsically positive or negative. We naturally feel our emotions and those feelings are not the same for each individual. Your job is to feel honestly and behave responsibly by expressing your emotions. It is your expression (or lack of expression) of the emotion that gives it a positive or negative "charge." Sometimes it is very positive to express anger: It would be appropriate to feel "MAD" if someone broke into your home.

And "GLAD" can carry negative energy; you probably do not benefit by expressing joy when a colleague is passed up for a promotion. If you are walking on the edge of a steep cliff, feeling "AFRAID" carries positive energy, for it causes you to be cautious and protect yourself.

Dual Emotions

Many feelings are associated with more than one of the basic emotions (MAD, SAD, GLAD, AFRAID.) You might feel "embarrassed." What emotion correlates with that feeling? No one can make this decision for you. It might feel like "mad" because you don't like the feeling of being judged; or it might be "afraid" because you fear that others might disapprove of your behavior.

You may feel "shame" and believe that you are "SAD." Look carefully at the feelings. Are you really "SAD," or might you feel "MAD" or "AFRAID?" It may be difficult at first to recognize fear, but it may be that you are "AFRAID" that someone may disapprove of your behavior. It is often difficult to see how much fear governs our lives.

Degrees of Feeling

Not all the feelings in the list carry the same energy. One person may feel "ecstatic," which would be at one extreme of "GLAD." Another may feel "okay," which would carry a lower energy for "GLAD." Both feelings fit under the basic emotion of "GLAD," but have a different intensity. Begin to define the intensity of the emotion. You might ask, "Did you feel a high level of "SAD" or a low level?"

Choosing our Emotions

It is easy to imagine (and really believe) that others cause our emotions. But your emotions are your own. You may not consciously choose to feel one way or another, but your past experiences led you to this emotion. Three individuals can experience virtually the same situation, and each might have a different emotional response.

Sometimes it is difficult to understand why someone who witnesses the same event does not feel the same as you do. It seems so clear-cut: "This situation is clearly sad." You may think, "How can anyone see it otherwise?" Each of us often operates out of our past, and since our experiences are different, our reactions also may be different. You have to ask yourself how you feel.

You may perceive that someone or something outside of yourself is causing your emotional state. You might say, "I feel irritated by his behavior." Why do you feel a sense of irritation? No one makes you feel a certain way. It is a choice—a reaction. This generally is very difficult to accept. It is much easier to look at another's irritating behavior than to look at your own reaction to their behavior. What a responsibility—owning your choice of emotional responses!

Sophia's Dream: A High Bed

Emotions: happy, full of anticipation (GLAD), reticent, unhappy (SAD), worried (MAD/AFRAID), reluctant, distraught, anxious, resigned (AFRAID), determined, courageous (OVERCOME FEAR/GLAD), distressed, unsafe, embarrassed, insecure, resistant (AFRAID), humble (GLAD)

I'm with a group having a class outdoors on a huge, very high bed, which must be eight to ten feet high. There are several mattresses piled on the four-poster bed to make it so high. There are no cushions or pillows on the bed; the cover is a golden brown, soft and fluffy like a duvet.

Everyone has already climbed up on it, and I'm reticent, hanging back. I don't like heights, and the thought of climbing up there makes me dizzy. If I do go up, that means I'll have to come down, and that's even worse.

I'm crying like a baby and stepping back and forth on my feet at the prospect of getting up, while the others call out to encourage me. I grapple the foot of the bed, pushing my fingers into layers of mattresses for a hold and search with my toes to get a footing as I pull myself up little by little. I don't look down in case I fall. The group bounces around, enjoying the view, I struggle to join them. They reach out to pull me onto the bed from the last step. My stomach turns over as I look down from this high platform. Ye Gads! There are no sides for protection! I feel totally ill at ease, unprotected, and unsafe. I feel sick to my stomach with the thought of climbing back down; don't think I can do it.

While doing our class work, someone leans towards me, pushing the mattress down, throwing me off balance. I tumble off the bed onto the ground. I am unhurt (except for my pride). The teacher checks to see if I'm all right, and two young men from our class help boost me back up on the bed.

∽∿

Belief System: Old Belief expressed in dream: You can't go, or you'll fall (fail). New Belief: I'm going there—with encouragement, someone's "lifting me up"—I'm in mid-air, feeling vulnerable—"out there" and it's ok.

This dream carried an unbelievable amount of fear in many forms: embarrassment, vulnerability, nausea, resistance, reticence, worry, distress, and resignation.

This is one of a few dreams I have had that remind me of a fairy tale or fable (like the Princess and the Pea). It draws my attention to really look for its message. I always in these cases research the originating fairy tale. The "pea" in this case was self-criticism, and the bed representing to me the layers of indecision and self-doubt I must let go of, in order to feel able to reach out for my dream in life. As I worked with the dream, I knew that I must face my extreme fears that held me back from reaching my goals. The feelings of vulnerability, of queasiness, are reminders of the challenging and daunting program I am about to embark on (DreamSynergy Certification). Luckily, I have lots of support to help me overcome my insecurities, as the dream reassures me.

DREAM SYNERGY
@@

Vocabulary of Emotions

+ GLAD -	+ SAD -	+ MAD -	+ AFRAID -
amusement	alienation	agitation	anxious
appreciation	boredom	angry	awe
awe	concern	annoyance	cautious
blissful	depression	anxious	concern
calm	devastation	betrayal	confusion
confident	disappointment	bitter	defensive
content	discouragement	confusion	desperate
delight	disgrace	critical	distress
ecstatic	dismal	deception	doubtful
energetic	defeat	disgust	embarrass
enthusiastic	distraught	dismay	frustration
excitement	exhaustion	displeasure	guilty
fortunate	hopeless	domination	helpless
fulfillment	hurt	enrage	hesitant
grateful	inadequate	envious	hopeless
happy	lonely	frustration	impatient
hopeful	gloomy	hostile	insecure
joyful	guilty	humiliation	intimidation
loving	miserable	impatient	jealous
OK	mournful	irritable	lonely
optimistic	neglect	jealous	nervous
passionate	regretful	offensive	overwhelm
relaxation	rejection	rage	regretful
relief	shame	rebellious	reluctant
respect	unhappy	repulsion	suspicious
secure	unlovable	resentful	timid
sensual	invalidation	ridicule	uncertain
spiritual	upset	sabotage	uncomfortable
thankful	weary	vindictive	vulnerable
tranquil	worthless	vengeful	worry

Physiological Response to Emotions

Have you awakened from a dream with heart racing, sweating, head pulsing? Your dreams often represent the true emotions you feel, although you have learned to ignore those emotions in your waking life. Our bodies carry the energy associated with our emotions. Often our health is negatively affected by this energy. It has been scientifically proven that *thinking* about being stabbed has an effect on your body similar to that resulting from an actual experience of *being* stabbed (psychogenic pain). Our bodies' response to the thought of being abandoned is similar to the response that occurs when one actually *is* abandoned. So if I believe that someone is going to do harm to me, that belief can affect me physiologically in a way that is similar to the response I would have experienced if he actually had done the harm. Whether a threat is real or merely perceived, the resulting fear can cause a racing heart, elevated blood pressure, or sweaty palms.

What emotions are you carrying in your body? Where do you carry them? Do you feel the emotional energy in your chest, your neck, your jaw, or your stomach? Learn to identify the emotional energy that you are carrying and proceed to help release the tension by deep breathing, meditating, and relaxing.

Many of us believe that we need to keep a tight lid on our emotions. We fear that if we ever allow these emotions to be expressed, they will do serious damage. But if we summon up the courage to truly feel our emotions, we discover that they don't last. The monster in the closet turns out to be a pussycat. In fact, if we are willing to experience our emotions completely, without resistance of any kind, they burn themselves out in only a few minutes. The only thing that keeps emotions alive within you over long periods is your unwillingness to acknowledge them.

By starving emotions we become humorless, rigid and stereotyped; by repressing them we become literal, reformatory and holier-than-thou. Encouraged, they perfume life; discouraged, they poison it.

—Joseph Collins

Exercise: Making Friends with Your Emotions

The following exercise may help you make a connection with the emotion itself and with the physiological state associated with the emotion. Make sure you have paper (preferably your dream journal) and pen handy as you work through the exercise. Rather than just thinking through the exercise, you will find that it is much more powerful and effective if you write your answers, especially in a journal where you can review them later.

After you have chosen a dream to honor, close your eyes and revisit the dream scene. Imagine the setting, characters, and action of the dream. Then ask yourself the following questions and write down your responses in your dream journal:

1. What are you feeling as you review the dream?
2. Which of the four basic emotions (MAD, SAD, GLAD, AFRAID) do you associate with that feeling?
3. What is the strongest emotion in the dream?
4. Where in your body do you experience your emotional response?
5. How do you react to each of these emotions in your body?
6. When do you feel this way in your waking life?
7. Is it a feeling that you want to nurture so you experience it often? If so, how can you do this? If it is not positive, how does this emotion affect your life?
8. If you feel any emotion right now, allow yourself to stay with it and feel it fully. What does this emotion remind you of in your life?

Journal about the impact of this emotion in your waking life.

Be aware of your emotions during the week ahead (both in your dreams and in waking life) and make note of the circumstances when you have feelings similar to the ones explored in this exercise. Note your physiological reactions to that emotion in waking life.

One of my dream group members, Sarah, found her voice through her dreams and dreamwork. She grew up in an alcoholic family where it was never safe to express herself honestly, and it was certainly not safe to express anger. When she became an adult, the unexpressed anger was turned on herself; she became severely depressed and seemed to be at the end of her rope. Her depression had not been relieved by traditional therapy or even at a treatment facility. The following dream and other dreams during this period of her life allowed her to believe that she could actually express her anger and survive! After hearing her dreams, the dream group encouraged her to begin sharing her honest emotions with her family. This was the beginning of her recovery from severe depression. As is frequently the case, her depression was caused by her turning her anger on herself instead of toward the appropriate persons.

Sarah's Dream: Finally Expressing Anger
Emotions: GLAD, MAD

I am in my early twenties and I am going out to dinner with my parents to a couple's home. I am going to reciprocate and ask them to our home the next weekend. Mother tells me I am not a good cook and I should not invite them over. She is very critical of me. I start screaming at her and tell her that I don't appreciate her treating me like that. I am very angry and not upset that I am angry.

99

Reflection: My inner child is developing angry feelings without guilt. I have always had a hard time expressing my anger, which has led to deep depression. The little girl is finally having a voice!

Focus on Characters

As you look at your dreams, you will begin to see characters who represent parts of yourself, acting and reacting in various ways. With the help of these dream characters, you can step back and perhaps for the first time see yourself more clearly. You can consider which of your qualities help you move forward, and which ones prevent you from achieving personal growth.

Dream characters often are represented as people you know, sometimes exhibiting their typical behaviors that you find irritating or distressing. You already know about those people and their habits, so why are you dreaming about them? It's a bummer to realize that a character's irritating behavior in your dream is actually shedding light on something about you. The good news is that the dream shows you this so that you can do something about it, and thereby become a happier, healthier person.

The dream is a gift from the unconscious, but so often we choose not to open that gift. After all, it is frightening to examine aspects of ourselves—both positive and negative, both golden shadow and dark shadow—that we have chosen to keep hidden away. In fact, often we do not *choose* to hide them because we are not even conscious that we have them. We just keep them in our unconscious, and often project the qualities onto others.

An unexamined dream is like an unopened letter from God.
—Talmud

When you look at the dream characters as aspects of yourself, you can see unmistakably how you treat yourself. When you review the dream and observe the dream action as your own creation, then you begin to take responsibility for your behavior. It may be (and often is) the first time you realize that you treat yourself in a particular way. You may begin to realize that you talk to yourself in negative ways and that you are often your own worst enemy—that you speak in the same negative way that voices from your past (parents, siblings, or teachers) used when they told you that you were wrong or not good enough.

Accepting this reality is difficult. We can easily perceive others' actions but are inept at recognizing our own reactions. If you tend to blame others for your predicaments, understanding yourself may help you stop blaming others for making your life miserable.

As you begin to recognize all these aspects of yourself, you will become more generally accepting of both yourself and of others. You become less critical and more aware of your reactions. You begin to understand the players in your game of life and view their actions objectively. You will no longer be caught up in being perfect, nor will you allow only your "good" parts to have a voice; you realize that in one way or another, the negative aspects will make themselves heard. If left unacknowledged, shadow aspects will express themselves, possibly in a passive-aggressive way. As you begin to see how you sabotage yourself and prevent yourself from reaching your full potential, you may realize how you sometimes are your own worst enemy—and perhaps your only "enemy!"

The dream gives you a glimpse of who you really are. As you begin to envision this more authentic way of being, you begin to act in ways that are consistent with it. The layers of camouflage that have been hiding your true Self begin to fall away. As you begin to act in an authentic way, others begin to treat you differently and eventually you are changed. You have begun to grow into the person your soul yearns to be.

James's Dream: Finding an Angel
Emotions: awe (GLAD), curious (GLAD/AFRAID), GLAD

I am walking to my car. Along the way, on the ground, I find a large gold silhouette cutout angel figure. It seems I've had it before, as I comment to it that it has come back to me.

ᕫᕬ

In a workshop dream group, James chose the angel symbol for the Dialogue with the Unconscious exercise.

Who are you? ... *A cherub.*
What should I call you? ... *Anaiel.*
Why are you here in my dream? ... *To re-connect with you.*
What do you want from me? ... *To use your gifts to the fullest.*
What do you know that I do not? ... *That you will be picking
    up/drawing things to you.*
What is the important thing you have to tell me? ... *Angels are a
    part of your life direction.*

James comments: I had never heard the name of this angel that came to me in my active imagination exercise, so I did some research. I discovered that Anaiel is considered to be the angel who taught knowledge to man (from the Book of Enoch).

In terms of how it supported me, the thing that comes to mind is that the dream acknowledged an intuitive ability to tap into angelic energies and discover that angels do exist in some form (maybe not the form that has been popularized); that somehow I had disconnected myself from that energy and it was coming back into my life again.

I think it might be more of a reclamation, as if I had an awareness of those qualities and then put some distance between them and myself; and then was ready to re-discover and reclaim them. The color gold makes me think of being the "golden child" growing up, the idea of always seeking ways to "shine," while at the same time seeking not to have the spotlight on me, not to be the center of attention. It is an interesting dichotomy.

Since the angel is a spiritual figure, finding it suggests reclaiming my spiritual nature, as I grew up quietly rebelling against formal, organized religion. I just felt I wasn't "cut out" to live life in the ways it was presented to me. It was just a matter of finding the path that was best suited to me.

It takes courage to begin to look at spiritual aspects of yourself, and especially to accept aspects of your nature that you have always viewed as negative in others.

People in my dream groups and workshops often are surprised that others like them more rather than less when they begin to be authentic and open. As you allow yourself to be more vulnerable, you become more approachable. As you allow yourself to be less "perfect," you become more human and available to others.

You may have heard people use the phrase "a part of me." For example, "A part of me really wanted him to get what was coming to him." As we look at our dreams and our waking life's actions and reactions, it is helpful to think about "parts of the self" that are childlike, parental, judgmental, bossy, driven, lazy, mature, etc. When you isolate and recognize each of these diverse aspects of yourself, you can appreciate that each is carrying out its own agenda and causing havoc—until you set some guidelines and bring them under control. This understanding can lead to a dramatic shift in your behavior.

We are quick to place "blame" on a character in a dream (just as we so often do in waking life). You might say, "My friend always acts like that. It makes me so mad. As in the dream, she is so critical of everything I do." It's always a wake-up call to ask, "So, what part of me does that remind me of? Is it the angry part, the joyful part, the sad part, or the scared part? How do I treat myself like that?" It's often hard for the dreamer to recognize this; it seems that the other character is the one causing the problem. I have been caught in this misconception and reminded by members of my dream group with the response, "So, what part of you acts like that?" It is often difficult to accept personal responsibility, even for the dream group leader!

Justina's Dream: Neglect our Baby Girl

Emotions: SAD, irresponsible (SAD), embarrassed (AFRAID), surprised (GLAD), SAD

I have forgotten about my baby girl. One night I remember her and realize I haven't fed her in a long time. I don't even know how she's surviving. I am amazed that she doesn't cry out more. She is quiet and has no energy.

I know I need to feed her. I love her but I certainly don't act like it. I decide to nurse her—I'm not sure I even have any milk. She starts to nurse and I'm surprised she remembers how, but she is really not interested and quits pretty quickly.

I call my friend. I realize it is three a.m. and I'm sure I woke her up. She doesn't say anything about the time of night or reprimand me. I feel terrible—I lost track of time. I apologize and am embarrassed.

Our little baby suddenly gets up out of my lap and walks. I am so surprised. I didn't know she could walk. Then she talks in complete sentences—more like a three-year-old. I'm surprised!

At the time I am totally focused on my husband who has had surgery and I'm waking up many times a night to check on him and help out. I am taking care of my mother, too, and concerned about my daughters. It seems like I am taking care of everyone but me.

This dream was a wake-up call to realize that I need to create time to take care of myself, especially my anima energy (baby girl).

Actually when I call the friend (part of myself that is better at focusing on my own needs), then my baby gains strength and the ability to express herself and walk on her own. This dream was very helpful in making me aware that I needed to remember to nurture myself in order to be strong enough to help others.

Exercise: Getting to Know You

I will give you an example of the exercise I used with the previous dream.

Close your eyes and move into your dream by observing the setting, action and characters.

1. Choose a character in the dream. *Friend*
2. List three characteristics of the character. *Responsible, pays attention to own needs and often puts them before others, thoughtful.*
3. Do you know a part of yourself that is or sometimes acts like that in life? Close your eyes and take on those aspects and feel that you are that person. *I know the responsible and thoughtful part but seldom the part that puts my own needs before others. I am getting more responsible to myself!*
4. It may be helpful to name this part of yourself so that you can relate to it (for example, The Boss, The Neglected Child, The Playful Partner). *The Caregiver of Myself*
5. When does this part of yourself take the lead in your waking life? *Usually only when I get sick or know that I am suffering because I am not being the "Caregiver of Myself."*
6. Go back into the dream and see the dream character acting in its particular way. Do you ever act this way? When? *I can easily see myself acting that way for a friend or family*

member, but I would generally feel like I should not bother someone else and interrupt his rest to help myself.

7. Journal about how this aspect of yourself hinders or supports your becoming the person you yearn to be. *I know that I cannot do the work I yearn to do and be the person I yearn to be without good health. I must take care of myself first and foremost, even though I was taught never to think of myself before others. I learned that well. I am getting much better with this behavior and being a caretaker to myself, but get negative "reviews" from my mother when I do. "How can you be so selfish?" Of course, I do realize it's often my own voice now questioning and judging. It's getting softer and quieter—and I am healthier!*

If you have time, go through the other characters in the same way—exploring and getting to know various aspects of your personality.

Awareness is the first step to change and individuation. In your waking life in the coming week, be aware of yourself acting and reacting like this dream character.

Justina's Dream: Tempted to Take Focus off Work
Emotions: Good (GLAD), honored (GLAD), slightly anxious (AFRAID), strong and committed (GLAD)

The board of an organization asked me to head up their annual gala with a couple of friends. I am flattered—what an honor!
I know it would be lots of fun, but I also know it would be very time-consuming. I am really busy with my dreamwork and enjoy it. I hesitate.

> *I tell them I personally don't think I can. I know my friends will probably do it. Part of me really wants to, but the more rational part says "NO." I know that I truly want to focus on my dreamwork.*
>
> ∾
>
> *Every now and then, I am tempted to take on another job that seems interesting. I could easily get off course from what I want to do with my time and life. My dreams come to remind me to stay focused and not add to my work so that I can impact the world of dreams, as well as enjoy time with family and friends.*
>
> *I was very proud of myself in the dream for resisting being pulled away by an honor and fun that would direct me away from the work I have at hand. The dream gave me the support and conviction to stay committed to my writing and dreamwork.*

Focus on Beliefs

Through your experiences in life, you have formulated certain beliefs. You consciously embrace some of your beliefs, but you may be less aware of other beliefs, and these can affect you in negative ways.

An example of a belief about which you are aware might be, "I am fortunate to have the opportunities I have been given." However, you might also believe, "I have to work hard and be miserable in order to be successful."

You may be aware of a set of beliefs that were passed down to you by your family, community, religion, and schools. Although you did not consciously choose these as your own beliefs, they affect your thoughts, words and actions—often without your even being aware of it. Some of these beliefs support the life you want to live and some of them prevent you from living that life. Often individual beliefs become part of a Belief System and this embedded system is more difficult to dissolve or change.

Many beliefs both support and interfere with living the life you wish to live. For instance, you may grow up believing that others are to be well respected and cared for. That belief can serve you well unless you take it to mean that you should take care of others at your own expense. Any belief taken to extreme can have negative effects on your life.

Often beliefs are unconscious—we are not aware that we are living by them. Since awareness is a very important agent for change, it is important to become conscious about all of our beliefs. Once you are aware of your beliefs, you can then examine them and choose whether you want to continue to live by them.

Some beliefs are appropriate when we are young, but as we mature they are no longer beneficial. We may be taught early that if we cross the street, we'll be run over. We learn later that we can cross a road without danger if we are careful, so we change that belief. It would be very restrictive to avoid crossing streets for the rest of your life. It is equally limiting to hang on to other old beliefs, especially an entrenched Belief System, without examining them.

Family Belief Systems often are passed down from generation to generation. They become mantras for our lives. We may believe them and accept them as truths without examination, even if they are dysfunctional. As adults we need to bring these Belief Systems to light and review them with a keen eye toward the values we hold dear and the life we choose to live.

For example, Joe grew up in a family that often expressed, "Big boys don't cry and are never afraid." He often felt sad and afraid, but knew that his family would not approve of him admitting it so he kept his emotions hidden. He learned to ignore his natural emotions and became numb even to his joy. It was by experiencing joy, sorrow, and fear in his dreams that Joe reclaimed his own emotional energy and, therefore, his true authentic nature.

It is important to realize that just because someone told you something in the past, it does not have to influence you now. You have the opportunity to make major changes and talk to yourself in supportive, positive ways.

It can be difficult to let go of a belief, no matter how irrational or dysfunctional it is. Think about it: If you get rid of it, what will you believe instead? To successfully eliminate an old, destructive belief, you must replace it with a new, supportive belief.

You have lived by and believed in the old messages throughout your entire life, so you must focus your attention on creating your new Belief System. Perhaps you believe that you are not worthy of having a happy life. You may not have been aware of self-defeating behavior, but nevertheless you may have managed to create a life that has not brought you any joy. A dream might offer a scenario in which you see these beliefs as part of a Cinderella type Belief System in action: "I don't deserve a happy life," "I am not smart enough to be successful," "I am not attractive." Once you define the beliefs that have been controlling your choices, you can consciously reject that system of beliefs and create a new one based on more supportive and honest beliefs about yourself. "I am worthy of having a happy life!" "I have not only intelligence and wisdom, but also skills to lead me to success." "I have an approachable and open personality that attracts people to me." Write the new beliefs down and keep them in view in order to establish this new Belief System as a mantra for your present and future.

Belief System

A pre-set, consistent (often unconscious) set of beliefs prevailing in a family, community or society.

The Belief System seems to be more ingrained in us than are individual beliefs. The system gives the individual belief a more fertile field in which to grow—feeding it in many different situations.

Remember that you have spent a lifetime believing and living out of the old Belief System, so be patient and intentional in learning your new supportive belief.

Justina's Dream: Homeless Intruder is My Teacher
Emotions: Anxious (AFRAID), furious (MAD)

I am with my husband in our house early one morning. We hear a noise downstairs. We look at each other; we are both slightly anxious. I say, "I think someone just came in our house."

Then we hear definite footsteps coming up the stairs. We are nervous. A disheveled man appears—not aggressive or upset.

I grab a yardstick and hit him over and over. My husband is just watching. I am yelling to get him to leave. My husband is right there but not helping as I usher the intruder to the living room and toward the window.

I'm pushing him over the back of the sofa and opening the window to push him outside. I am furious! It's hard to get him out. I yell to my husband, "CALL POLICE!"

There are some neighbors yelling at me. They say that he's not dangerous and that they no longer call the Police on him—that he's homeless and lives in the neighborhood, that he's harmless as far as they can tell.

I say, "Well, he shouldn't come in someone's house without permission!" I also ask them why I haven't been notified about him.

My husband is silent throughout. It is all very stressful to me.

℮⁄☉

I wrote out an Active Imagination the next morning:

Who are you? *I am an intruder. I am in your house because I thought you needed me.*

For what? *To help you understand simple things and to appreciate all you have.*

What can you teach ME? *I have little—not even a home—and my days are good. I enjoy the beauty of each day. I am not anxious. I am provided for.*

YOU are a BUM! *You may call me that. I choose to think of myself as a man with few needs and many blessings.*

Like what? *Well, I don't have the anxiety you carry—you always desire more. Not so much material goods, but more accomplishments, more accolades. It's endless for you.*

How do I change that? *I came to help you but you used your energy to get me out of your living space, hitting me with a measuring stick because I didn't measure up to your standards. I have standards, too—just not yours! I don't hurt anyone and I don't expect anyone to take care of me. I just exist in the midst of all—hopefully invisible. Every now and then I have to make myself visible to get someone's attention. I hope you'll invite me back in someday.*

I was deeply touched by the words that came from that voice of the "intruder." It was true, and it made me pause to ask myself what I really want and need in my life at the present time. Back to my journal for a fuller "talk with myself" to make sure I am living my life as I yearn to live it. I no longer want to live out of an old belief that says "I have to accomplish great things and be productive in order to be worthy of respect." My new belief would be "Being fully authentic and enjoying each day is enough." My cat Schatzi is a great teacher of that belief.

If you have children, have a discussion about family beliefs. Allow the children to speak their truth and reflect on the systems set up by generations before them. You may learn a lot from the younger generation. And your children will learn a lot from your openness.

Dreams will help you see your beliefs in a new way. You can actually view how the belief supports or sabotages you in your life. You can view characters acting and reacting out of various systems of belief, and apply that observation to your personal life. Your life will change in a constructive way when you are aware of the beliefs that influence you and your decisions. Now you will be able to make more positive and supportive decisions based on your new updated beliefs.

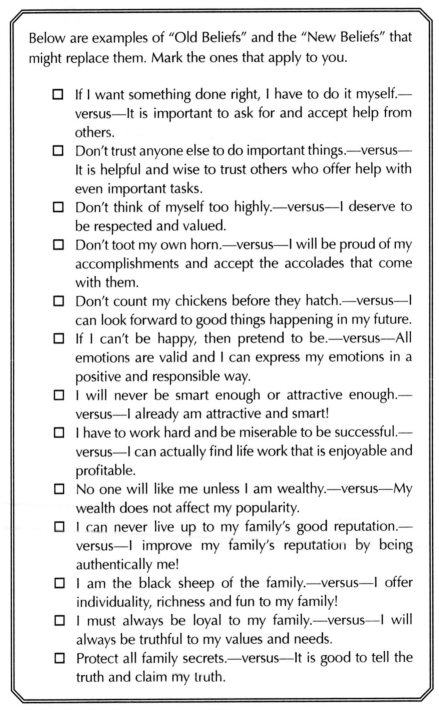

Below are examples of "Old Beliefs" and the "New Beliefs" that might replace them. Mark the ones that apply to you.

- ☐ If I want something done right, I have to do it myself.—versus—It is important to ask for and accept help from others.
- ☐ Don't trust anyone else to do important things.—versus—It is helpful and wise to trust others who offer help with even important tasks.
- ☐ Don't think of myself too highly.—versus—I deserve to be respected and valued.
- ☐ Don't toot my own horn.—versus—I will be proud of my accomplishments and accept the accolades that come with them.
- ☐ Don't count my chickens before they hatch.—versus—I can look forward to good things happening in my future.
- ☐ If I can't be happy, then pretend to be.—versus—All emotions are valid and I can express my emotions in a positive and responsible way.
- ☐ I will never be smart enough or attractive enough.—versus—I already am attractive and smart!
- ☐ I have to work hard and be miserable to be successful.—versus—I can actually find life work that is enjoyable and profitable.
- ☐ No one will like me unless I am wealthy.—versus—My wealth does not affect my popularity.
- ☐ I can never live up to my family's good reputation.—versus—I improve my family's reputation by being authentically me!
- ☐ I am the black sheep of the family.—versus—I offer individuality, richness and fun to my family!
- ☐ I must always be loyal to my family.—versus—I will always be truthful to my values and needs.
- ☐ Protect all family secrets.—versus—It is good to tell the truth and claim my truth.

- ☐ Real men don't show emotions.—versus—It is beneficial for all people to express emotions.
- ☐ Don't ever be afraid!—versus—Expressing fear is healthy and beneficial to my well being.
- ☐ The early bird gets the worm.—versus—Sometimes even better worms are available later in the day.
- ☐ Family is always more important than friends.—versus—Friends are family that we get to choose.
- ☐ Don't let anyone see my vulnerabilities.—versus—Be authentic and open, allowing others to see who I truly am.
- ☐ Always think of others before myself.—versus—I cannot care for others unless I care for myself first.
- ☐ Never let others down.—versus—Sometimes my own needs are more important to meet than another's.
- ☐ My parents always know what is best for me.—versus—Often, I am the only person who knows what is best for me.
- ☐ What I am upset about is never worthy of tears.—versus—Crying is an honest and healing expression of my emotions.
- ☐ Early to bed, early to rise, makes a man healthy wealthy and wise.—versus—A good and restful night's sleep is important to my health and well being.
- ☐ Go to my room and come out smiling.—versus—It is ok to show my emotions in a non-threatening way.
- ☐ Don't wear my heart on my sleeve.—versus—It is sometimes beneficial to show others that I care deeply for someone else.
- ☐ Don't take things so seriously.—versus—Some things are important to me and should be taken seriously.
- ☐ Always do my very best!—versus—Do what needs to be done for the particular job; "perfect" is not always required.
- ☐ I am accountable, so I must always have the right answer!—versus—Be accountable, but accept that I will not always make the "perfect" decision.

Exercise: What Are My Beliefs?

Do you have your dream journal for recording your answers? I'll wait—you can go get it.

- List beliefs that you were taught and may continue to hold as truth.
- Do those beliefs serve you? If not, why are you still living your life with them at the center?

Exercise: What Do You Choose to Believe?

The following exercise will help you begin to recognize and review beliefs that affect your life.

Review the dream you choose to honor.

1. Make a vertical list of the characters in the dream, leaving space after each character's "name."
2. After each character, write a belief from which the character operates. (Do this fairly rapidly. Often the first thought is the best in dreamwork.)
3. What is the main belief that controls the action (or outcome) of the dream?
4. Note which of these beliefs are part of your behavior in your life. Do you think each is valid?
5. Who taught you these beliefs?
6. Do those beliefs improve the quality of your life?
7. How do any of your beliefs—exemplified by the dream— keep you from making positive movement in your life?
8. If you want to move beyond that belief, how might you transform it into a new belief? Write the new belief on an index card and keep it visible during the next few weeks.

Remember that you did not learn the old belief in one day—nor probably even one year—and you will not change it in a day, either. Be consistent in reminding yourself of your new supporting belief.

Levels of Exploration: Recap, Relationship, and Recognition

I encourage you to go to the deepest level (Recognition) in your dreamwork, but you will change even by just dipping your toe into the waters of dreamwork at the first level (Recap). Remember that even dreaming without recall achieves a benefit psychologically. You can't lose, but you do have a choice about how much you want to gain from the gift of your dreams. Start with awareness of your dreams, move to looking more closely at your dreams, then at your relationships in your dreams, and then to recognizing your own responsibility for your thoughts, reactions, and emotions.

Recap

Even at its most superficial level, your dream exploration can offer benefits. You may believe that a particular dream is merely a recap of the previous day's events. It is true that some dreams feature characters, occurrences, and details similar to those you have experienced recently in waking life. But a resemblance to waking life events is no reason to dismiss the potential for exploring the dream!

Look closely at the dream and compare it to the daily events you think it resembles. What is different? What new information does the dream offer? Does the dream include a character that was not present in waking life the day before? Is the dream setting different from the places where you spent the previous day? For example, you may have a dream that is similar to an experience of being at a bank the previous day. You almost dismiss it as a replay of a waking life event, but then remember to look more deeply at the dream. You notice that in the dream the teller is your sister rather than the person who actually waited on you. What is your sister trying to tell you? (She is taking the role of the "teller.") Have you been ignoring her words that are warning you about not taking care of your health? Perhaps she is giving you something that will provide the most important information for your future. Pay attention to everything in your dreams!

Remember: The dream does not come to you in order to waste your time with information you already have. It calls you to listen and watch more intently and to gather information you may have missed in waking life events.

Relationship

At the second level, you can examine the dream in terms of your relationships with others. By exploring the energy and emotions represented in a dream, you can experience the intensity of emotions and energy within a particular waking-life relationship. By examining and understanding what is truly happening in your life, you have an opportunity to make positive changes in your personal relationships.

Recognition

The third level is where your deepest work is accomplished. This is where information from the unconscious moves into consciousness. View the role of each dream character as an aspect of yourself. By recognizing and accepting them as your own, you will begin to accept responsibility for your life.

You begin to see more clearly how you affect all of the events and relationships of your life. It is a difficult place to go, for you will understand that you must take responsibility for your own life. This is the point in dreamwork where life changes can be made!

Melissa's Dream: Resisting Fun at the Beach
Emotions: ok (GLAD), hesitant (SLIGHTLY AFRAID, SAD), jealous (AFRAID, SAD)

I'm at the beach sitting on the shore with my husband. There are lots of people in the water. I am tempted to go into the ocean but hesitate, knowing that it will then require me to wash my hair and that I won't get to read my book I brought.

The people in the water all seem to be enjoying themselves, jumping and riding the waves, laughing and playful.

My husband knows that I would like to go into the ocean and kids me about not going. "Why don't you go? Are you afraid you'll get wet or tossed under by a wave?"

There are many people nearby on the shore sunning, talking, and reading.

Recap Level:

Melissa had been at the beach recently and had a similar experience of wanting to go into the ocean, but not for the same reasons as in the dream.

What was different in the dream was the emotional energy Melissa felt. She said she really felt anxious and sad. She started to dismiss the dream as a "replay" of an actual event until she remembered to pay attention to the emotions and scene of the dream.

After answering the questions in the "Making Friends with Your Emotions" exercise, Melissa realized that she felt anxiety and sadness about joining in the fun of swimming. She didn't realize how her hesitation to "join in" affected her emotionally and physically in waking life. Her chest and throat felt tight as she remembered the dream. The day before there was too much activity on the beach for her to even notice that response.

Now Melissa was able to ask herself, "Why did I feel so much anxiety and sadness in my dream?" That took her to the second level of dream exploration.

Relationship Level:

Melissa first focused on the behavior of her husband in reality and in the dream.

"He made fun of me for not going. He judged me rather than supporting or encouraging me. I realized that he does this often and I try to shrug it off, but for the first time I was consciously aware of how I felt judged and laughed at by him. Wow, it really does cause physiological responses in my body!"

When reviewing the dream, Melissa also noticed that in the dream, her friend Paula is sitting near her on the beach. In waking life the day before, this friend had not been at the beach. In the dream, Paula was reading, but jumped up to join others and, as she was heading to the ocean, called out to Melissa to join her. "It's amazing how I had ignored that part of the dream since it didn't really happen in waking life."

Melissa decided to share this dream with her husband. It seemed like a good opportunity to discuss how his critical comments affect her. It seemed easier to talk about the issue through a dream and he seemed more receptive. Once he knew that the remarks felt demeaning to his wife, he promised that he would try harder to be supportive and not so judgmental. This created an opening in their relationship that allowed healing and more intimacy.

Recognition Level:

When Melissa was ready, she took the dream to a deeper, more transforming level, and did the "Getting to Know You" exercise.

She looked at the characters as aspects of herself. She knew that her husband could be judgmental, unaware of emotions, and focused on himself. When she looked at those characteristics within herself—"judgmental, emotionless, and self-centered"—she realized that they were factors when she criticized herself, which was often. She did not focus on herself when it came to choices and priorities, but she admitted that she was very self-conscious. She considered the question in the dream: "Why don't you go? Are you afraid you'll get wet or tossed under by a wave?" She was then able to see how she often questioned herself in the same way. This was the reason her husband's words often cut deeply and created such pain for her. She realized that she already opened wounds with her self-judgment, and his remarks rapidly cut to the quick.

Melissa considered the characteristics of her friend/dream character Paula: kind, risk-taker, independent. She looked closely at those aspects of herself, and recognized them in her own personality, but admitted that they were most often overruled by her critical inner voice.

By exploring the dream through Active Imagination (see Dialogue with the Unconscious exercise in Chapter 4), she looked at both parts of herself that the dreamwork had brought to consciousness. In the exercise, she made a deal to give the supportive voice more power than the judgmental voice. This led her to the realization that she often sabotaged her own growth and individuation.

Melissa said, "I was aware for the first time how I allowed that critical voice within to rule my life—especially new and fun adventures."

She questioned what belief supported the criticism toward taking risks and fully enjoying life? She dove into the exercise "What Do You Choose to Believe?" It took her only seconds to recognize the belief: "Hard work and dependable behavior are the most important aspects of a person's character." She continued to ask where she learned that and quickly realized, "From my Dad!" She came to the conclusion that she no longer wanted that belief to control her life. Her new belief would be, "All work and no play makes Jack (and Melissa) a dull person!"

In reviewing the dream, the setting is important as well. The ocean often represents the unconscious in its depth and breadth. Melissa asked herself if she was hesitant in her waking life to really cast herself into the new work she was studying in the field of dreams. She realized that she felt safer sitting on the shore and reading a book about dreams.

While thinking about the setting, she also realized that on the shore she had a much wider perspective than she does in her busy, crowded life. "What a perfect event for my dream-maker to use in order to help me move to new understanding and potential change! I understood in a different way, at a deeper level, and now I had a choice to move ahead on my path of personal growth!"

Wake Up! DreamSynergy™ can help you reach your waking dreams and desires by giving you simple guidelines to following your nighttime dreams. Do you understand the impact of your emotions? Is fear preventing you from becoming all that you are born to be? Are you using your beliefs as excuses to keep you from getting what you say you most want? What characters (parts of yourself) are keeping these beliefs alive?

CHAPTER 6

⊚⊚

Discover Your Greatest Potential through Dreamwork

I have had dreams and I have had nightmares, but I have conquered my nightmares because of my dreams.

—Jonas Salk

Each dream beckons the dreamer to see its message in a new light. Dreamwork is at its best when you use a variety of methods and techniques. The exercises in this chapter are designed to guide you toward the "gold" in the dream. They "turn up the volume" on various aspects of the dream material so that the dream's message will be more accessible to you.

- Please pay very careful attention to the dream content and the emotions of the dream. Be aware of how it impacts you regarding emotions, characters, beliefs, settings, color, symbols, metaphors, etc.
- After recording and reading through your dream, take a few minutes to absorb the images, emotions, and action in the dream. Then proceed with the in-depth work using one of the exercises in this chapter.
- Listen carefully for metaphors and unusual symbolic language, and look for symbols and powerful images.
- Be aware of your own physiological responses. What are you feeling as you remember your dream? Where do you feel it in your body?

- If your mind wanders, note the point at which you stopped paying attention to the process. This is often where a personal issue has surfaced for you.

One exercise may inspire you to make up another exercise of your own. Use this as a "jumping off" point for your work. Continue the process intuitively—trust yourself to "know without knowing." Where does the dream lead you?

If you were sitting with me working with your dreams, I might ask you some of the following questions. Get together with a friend and lead each other through the DreamSynergy™ method. Choose a dream exercise that you want to use before you begin the dreamwork process that follows.

Practice a DreamSynergy™ Dreamwork Session

You may want to tell or read the dream aloud (preferably to someone else, but possibly using a tape recorder). When you say the dream aloud, you hear it differently, as if someone else is hearing it and reflecting on your words. Listen and speak with an open mind and heart. Try to stay out of your "thinking mind."

1. What part of the dream draws your attention? Where is the greatest energy or emotion in the dream? Where do you feel that energy in your body?
2. If there is another area of tension or pleasure, check that feeling out with your body.
3. Close your eyes and say aloud again that part of the dream that carries the greatest energy or emotion, with all the details that you can garner.
4. With eyes closed, look around in the dream. Are there any additional details, objects, characters that you did not notice or remember previously?
5. Do you have any immediate connections to your waking life?
6. Look at the setting(s) of the dream. Do you recognize any of those places in your waking life? In a few words, what do they represent to you? Do they impart positive or negative feelings? (In the dream? In waking life?)

---

7. Consider the action of the dream. What is trying to be accomplished in the dream?
8. What either facilitates that happening or prevents that from happening? How is that represented in your waking life?
9. Connect the emotions and physiological responses. What are you feeling emotionally right now?
10. Where do you feel that energy in your body? Close your eyes and be aware of that feeling.
11. What is the main emotion (GLAD, MAD, SAD, or AFRAID) that you associate with that feeling?
12. If you feel any emotion (GLAD, MAD, SAD, AFRAID), allow yourself to stay with it and feel it fully. What does this emotion remind you of in your waking life?
13. What is the theme or synopsis of the dream? Try to write this in as few words as possible.
14. How do you connect this theme to your waking life?
15. How would you "ritualize" your dream? Create an action that honors your dream in some way. Find an object that will remind you of your dream and place it where you can see it often. Or take time to actually do something that was enjoyable in the dream. This will help imprint the dream in your mind and body and help move you to a fuller understanding of the dream. For example, I continually dream of art and creative activities, so I arranged for a day of art with my grown daughters. I contracted with Tammy Papa, an artist whose work I admire, to lead us in a day of pastels painting. We had such fun! I recharged my "Artist" and was very proud of my accomplishments and commitment to my creativity. As another example, a mother bear played an important role in one of my dreams, so I put a little toy bear on my kitchen windowsill to remind me of the dream's message.

Keep your dream alive in the coming week (and beyond) and embrace all that it has to teach.

Be aware of your actions in the week ahead. Do you act like any of the negative or positive characters in the dream? Do you hear the sabotaging voice? Stop and change that message to one that is based on your new belief system.

Paul's Dream: Grasshopper Gummy Bears
Emotions: free, optimistic (GLAD)

I am in a bathroom. It is dark. The only object visible is the bathtub, which is empty. I am standing over the tub. I see scurrying out, through a tiny crack in the wall near the faucet, many grasshopper-shaped gummy bears. They move as quickly as they can to get out from behind the wall, and scurry down the wall to the top of the tub. Then they move along the top end of the tub in a slow steady march forward. Then they make a right turn and move steadily forward along the top of the tub on long side of the tub.

They are not hopping like grasshoppers. Their shape is soft and smooth; no rough edges. They are about two inches long, much too big to get through a tiny hole in the wall. They are bright shades of lime green and they are translucent. The bathroom is dark except that the gummy bear grasshopper's glow (they are sort of fluorescent). They are not scary, ugly bugs. They are playful looking and non-threatening.

They don't fall into the tub or over the side. As I observe this scene, I am puzzled by them. They are very curious critters. I don't know what to do. How do I stop them? Should I even try to stop them? There are so many.

☙❦

Paul's Process: Justina acted as a guide to help me interpret the dream. I sat in a comfortable chair in front of her in her comfortable chair. She took notes and gave them to me at the end of the session so that I would not be distracted by taking my own notes. Often she asked me to close my eyes to focus better on the dream.

I started by describing the dream. She asked me to describe the emotions of the dream (MAD, SAD, GLAD, or AFRAID). She then asked me to close my eyes and try to give more detail. That now is all contained above in my description of the dream. She noted that I called them gummy bear grasshoppers and asked what "bears" symbolize to me. I said "soft and cuddly and full of hugs."

In response to her question about the color in the dream, I said lime green was the color of spring, growth, freshness, and renewal. I added that though the objects were in the shape of a grasshopper they didn't actually hop but moved at a steady quick pace along the side of the tub. Like an army of ants, as if nothing could stop them. They didn't seem to have any destination. They just kept moving forward with confidence.

Then she asked me to close my eyes again and pretend I was the grasshoppers and describe my emotions as a grasshopper. I said, "I want to get out from behind the wall and into the light and air. I am fun and playful. I am lots of bright colors of green. I dislike being behind that dark wall. I am playful and enjoy my freedom."

As the gummy bear, I feared some big person will squash me. She asked who that might be and what belief I held that would support that fear. I wasn't sure, so I theorized that it could be my wife (or her lawyer), or women I date, and that I could get hurt in a relationship again. Later I added "death" as another possibility (the night before I called a good friend to give my condolences regarding the death of her brother). I said I would have such a long list of unfinished business if I died. I also told Justina that as a gummy bear grasshopper I am soft, cute, sweet, and playful, almost irresistible. No one would have any reason to squash me. I knew I felt free and alive when I came out from behind the dark wall, and I know that grasshoppers only leap forward!

As we went through this process as some of my feelings came out, it brought tears to my eyes. (I try to prevent that from happening in my waking life. Dreams seem to reach that deep place for me!)

Here is how I would summarize the learning from the dream:

Behind the dark wall was my marriage, or at least my prior life. I scurry through the tiny hole in the wall, which is extremely difficult, because I am desperate to emerge from behind the wall to be alive and free. Once I get through the hole, I always move forward at a steady pace. I am playful and fun and sweet and colorful and fascinating. People want me—they want to stick to me, and I want to stick to them. I am "translucent," meaning that I am open and honest with people. I don't hide anything. The bathtub symbolizes pleasure for me.

The grasshoppers are skirting around the edges on top of the tub. The grasshoppers are not afraid and not in danger in this forward march. They are too irresistible for anyone to want to squash them.

There are too many of them. If you squash one, more come out from behind the wall to replenish. They have no particular goal. They just keep marching forward at a steady pace.

In looking at new understanding from the dream message for my life, I said the dream mostly was an extremely positive reinforcement that I am doing the right thing in dissolving my marriage and moving forward. If there was any new learning, it is the fear of getting squashed. They continue to move forward. Even if one part of me gets hurt, the many other parts will be happy to have emerged from behind the wall.

Summary: The dream is about freedom—coming out from behind a dark wall; and my unrelenting march forward without looking back. I left the session with a new confidence and belief that I am moving forward in my life in a positive direction!

The Ritual: I bought a package of green gummy bears and enjoyed each one in a mindful, joyful way.

DREAM SYNERGY
Dreamwork Exercises

Choose a dream exercise offered in the following pages and look at your dream in that way.

Or ask a friend to listen to your dream, and ask her what it would mean to her if *she* had the dream. It is not for her to tell you what it means for you! That is impossible since she hasn't lived your life. Ask her to use an "If it were my dream ..." response format.

Write in your journal about your reflections on the dream and your life.

As you do these exercises, remember the advice given earlier in this chapter:

- Listen carefully for metaphors and unusual language, and look for symbols and powerful images.

- Be aware of your own physiological responses. What are you feeling as you remember your dream? Where do you feel it in your body?
- If your mind wanders, note the point at which you stopped paying attention to the process. This is often where a personal issue has surfaced for you.

Many of the following exercises can be done both individually and within a group setting. Some of the exercises are simpler and easier than others. None of the exercises is too simple for even the most experienced dreamer. I find some of the simplest ones provide just the message I need.

After working with your dream, it is important to carry the new learning over to your waking life. It is in repeating and incorporating the messages into your daily life that you will begin to make positive shifts. Remember that you probably learned the negative, sabotaging behavior over your entire life. How many years is that? Keep the dream alive, give yourself the message over and over, and allow the message to continue growing and expanding.

Some ways to keep your dreams alive:

- Work with your dream using several of the exercises below. You can always gain new wisdom from a dream; the possibilities never seem to be exhausted. I really believe that you can take one dream and gain meaning from it throughout your life. That is how powerful dreams are!
- Write the new message you gain from your dreamwork on an index card in large letters, creating a new "mantra" for you to use. Put it where you see it often. Remember: You are teaching yourself new beliefs about yourself and the world.

- Choose an interesting dream character to ride in your car with you for a week. Give the character the front passenger seat and imagine conversations with him throughout the week. It's best to do this when you are alone, so that others will not question your sanity—and don't let it interfere with your attention to safe driving. (Especially good if you spend lots of time in the car. I did this a lot when I drove carpool for my children all day!)

Montague Ullman, M.D.

Dream enthusiasts owe much to Montague Ullman, M.D., a psychiatrist and psychoanalyst (1916 – 2008) who laid the foundations for much of present-day group dreamwork. Dr. Ullman promoted public interest in dreamwork in the 1970s and advocated the importance of safety and discovery in the dreamwork process. He proposed the use of "If it were my dream," which is a vital part of successful group dreamwork. I suggest you study the techniques in his book, *Appreciating Dreams: A Group Approach.*

Exercise: A Quick Look at a Dream

Sometimes there is no time to write down your dreams in the morning. Here is a shortcut when time is of the essence.

1. What is trying to be accomplished in the dream?
2. How is this accomplished, or what prevents it from happening?
3. What do you feel emotionally in the dream?

4. How do you connect any of this to your waking life?
5. What can you learn from this?

Answering these questions takes only a few minutes and can be done without recording the entire dream story. Try it with one of your dreams.

Exercise: Emotional Check-In

Some people who are not adept at knowing what they are feeling may need to take an "emotion break" along with a coffee break and ask, "How do I feel right now?"

1. Make copies of the Vocabulary of Emotions (VOE) chart. Keep it with you throughout the day. Several times during each day, stop and ask, "What am I feeling right now?"
2. Look at the VOE and circle the words within the list that best describe how you are feeling at the moment.
3. At the end of the week, note which column contains most of your circled words and therefore most of your emotional energy for that week. Do this for several weeks.

It is enlightening to note over the course of a week which words in the chart are most often recognized and marked. This may be the first time you have seriously looked at emotions in your life. It's all about awareness!

Eventually you will be able to articulate an emotion without using the chart, be closer to understanding how you feel, and have a better foundation for your decisions and actions.

Exercise: Dream Characters

This exercise is an alternate way of looking at dream characters. Like some of the previous exercises, it helps you begin to get to know and understand dream characters as aspects of yourself.

Choose a character from your dream. Ask the following questions and record your answers:

1. Describe this character's personality. What are this character's main characteristics? Be aware of what the character is wearing, how he/she is positioned, what he/she is feeling.
2. Imagine you are playing the role of this character. Become aware of how the character feels in the dream. What are the basic emotions the character feels now?
3. What does this character want?
4. How do you feel about this character? What emotions does he/she invoke?
5. Do you see this character as friend or foe?
6. Does this character see him/herself as your friend or foe?
7. Does this character see you as his/her friend or foe?
8. Do you recognize this character as a part of your personality?
9. What does this character have to teach you?
10. How does this character support you in a positive way, or sabotage you in waking life? Remember that this character represents part of your own personality.

Journal: What lessons can you learn from this character's perspective?

Exercise: Look at Personal Beliefs

The following exercise will help you begin to recognize and review belief systems that affect your life.

1. Review the dream you choose to honor.
2. Make a vertical list of the characters in the dream, leaving space following each character's "name."
3. After each character, write a belief from which the character operates. (Do this fairly rapidly. Often the first thought is the best in dreamwork.)
4. What is the main belief that controls the action (or outcome) of the dream?
5. Note which beliefs are part of your behavior in your life. Do you think each is valid?
6. Who taught you these beliefs?
7. Do they improve the quality of your life?
8. How do any of the beliefs of the dream prevent you from making positive movement in your life?

Create new beliefs to substitute for the old beliefs that no longer benefit your life. Write them on an index card, and keep the card where you can see it often during the next few weeks.

Exercise: Draw the Dream

It is hard to translate all the essence of a dream into words. Drawing dreams is a good way to bypass the limitations of words. The impact of the dream is much greater than the individual elements of the dream. Sometimes we have to move to words to think as we acquire knowledge and understanding, but the emotions and energy associated with dream images provide the real information for change and transformation. What do you feel about the images of your dreams? What memories are stirred up?

☺/☺

Use your non-dominant hand and have no preconceived idea of what you are going to draw. Let the dream lead the way. Using your non-dominant hand allows you to connect with a more creative, less judgmental part of your thinking. (Compared to the non-dominant hand, the dominant hand seems to be controlled by an area of the brain that is much more "critical" and connected to the ego's agenda.) Workshop participants are amazed at the knowledge that arises out of a drawing that is created without the control available in the dominant hand. For me, my non-dominant hand has not been trained as an artist, so I don't have the same expectations of my drawing being "good." It allows me to be more spontaneous and open—not trying to create a work of art, but instead a feeling of the dream.

Once the drawing is complete, view the drawing as if you are on a treasure hunt, looking for clues:

1. Are there any predominant colors? Did you use only one color or many? Did you choose not to use color?
2. What is the largest object in the picture? What is the smallest?
3. Look at the placement of the objects in the drawing. What is in the center of the page?
4. What part of the page does your drawing occupy? Did you extend the drawing to the edges of the paper?
5. Who is in the picture? Are the other characters depicted in your drawing people you actually know in waking life?

6. Where are you in the drawing? Are you inside or outside of the action? Are you observing or participating? Did you "leave yourself out of the picture?" Do you do that in your life?

7. Are you surprised by the inclusion or exclusion of any dream images?

8. Is anything incorporated into the drawing that was not written in your dream?

9. Are there any symbolic designs in the drawing: circles, triangles, spirals, crosses, stars, etc.? (Information about the symbolism of these shapes can be found in many books listed in the Suggested Reading section at the end of this book.)

Show your drawing to someone and ask what he/she sees in your drawing before you tell him/her about your dream.

Now place your drawing where you will see it often. You will continue to garner new meaning as you reflect on it.

Exercise: Amplify Color

I am intrigued by color work because it relates so well to the meaning of the dream. Color truly amplifies the emotions and energy.

You may not be aware of color in the dream until you pay close attention. (See Chapter 4 for more information on color.)

It's fun to work with color. It is still such a surprise even to me that color ties in so closely to the message of the dream. How can we be so clever and creative?!

1. Re-read the dream and recall as many colors as you can.

2. Include colors that are not written in your dream journal, but that you notice in the dream. (You may know that a house in the dream was yellow, but may not have recorded it. This is an important distinction. It could have been a red brick house!)
3. Is one color predominant in the dream?
4. How does the color amplify the meaning of the image to which it is associated? Write in your dream journal any insight you have gained.

As you become aware of the importance of color in uncovering the meaning, you will grow more aware of color in your dreams. Pay attention to color in future dreams and note it and add color to your dream sketches.

Suggested references on color are: *The Herder Dictionary of Symbols*, Wilda B. Tanner's *The Mystical, Magical, Marvelous World of Dreams*, and Robert J. Hoss's *Dream Language: Self-Understanding through Imagery and Color.*

⊚ ⊚ ⊚

Exercise: Who Am I Becoming?

We need to focus on who we are becoming. Your beliefs about yourself change in your dreams before they do in your waking life. Your dreams will give a clearer vision of how you are living your life. The dream may say, "Well done," or "Get on with your personal growth."

1. Read over the last three dreams you have had.
2. Write the adjectives describing the person you are in each dream.

3. How would you appear to an outsider? (Calm, responsible, anxious, attractive, shy, etc.?)

4. Which adjectives do you most identify with? Which do you identify with least?

5. Can you see yourself as that person? Do you identify with the ways you act like that person in your waking life?

6. How do you envision yourself in the future? Write a description. Close your eyes and envision that person.

7. Write a vision of your future self on an index card and put it where you can see it often. It is a glimpse into your future. Actually you already have those attributes—you just need to claim them. You already are what you yearn to be.

Exercise: Explore House Dreams

 Many dreams contain images of houses or buildings— everything from simple tents to magnificent castles. We can use these dream images to uncover additional meanings of the dream. A house often represents the psyche (see the Glossary for definition), and observations of yourself can be made in relation to the house or building. For instance, when looking at the structure or the foundation of a house in your dream, ask "What is the structure of my psyche?" or "What supports my life?"

1. Write a description of the house (or building) in the dream, giving as much detail as possible. Describe the landscape surrounding the house and the condition of the house.

2. If the dream only contains the interior of the house, describe in detail the appearance of the room(s) and the furnishings.

3. Answer some of the questions below and relate to aspects of yourself. Think in terms of the symbolic and metaphorical language of the dream.

4. How do you enter the house? Is there a door? Is it open or locked? Do you enter through the front or back door? Think of these questions in terms of your personal availability to others (and perhaps to yourself). Are you "open" to yourself and others, or do you keep yourself "locked up?" Are you available to people in general, or do you limit your interactions to those you know well? Who and what must approach you via the front door (more formally), and who/what is close and comfortable enough to be welcome through the back door?

5. Are there windows? Do the windows allow a clear view or are they covered? What is the view from the house? (What is your waking perspective of the situation? Can you see clearly?)

6. What is the structure of the house? Is it well made? Is there a foundation? What is the condition of the foundation? (Evaluate your personal "structure." Do you have the support you need? Do you have a good foundation?)

7. Is the house spacious or small and cramped? Are there individual rooms or large open spaces? Is there more than one floor? (How do you feel in this space? Is this a familiar feeling in your waking life?)

8. Is the style Victorian, contemporary, or modern? Is it a castle, apartment, mansion, or haunted house? Does the house remind you of a familiar house in your life? (The style of house often relates to your history; for example, when did this "issue" begin? Did this occur in the time of

your grandparents or is it part of your contemporary life or part of your future?)

9. Have you recently moved or are you moving into the house? Are you surprised by the magnificence of the house? (Perhaps you are "moving" your life to claim the treasures that you are gifted.)

10. What is the condition of the house? Is there anything wrong with the house? Is it open to the elements? Is everything intact? Is the house precariously perched? (Compare this to your waking life "condition.")

11. Is the house under construction or renovation? What is being done to the building? How major is the work that needs to be done? Do you need to remodel just one room or tear down the entire structure? Are you considering touch-up paint, or is that just delaying the necessary work? (Perhaps you are under "renovation" or need to be.)

12. Does the house need major house cleaning or organizing? (Do things need organizing in your life? Does clutter prevent you from moving forward into your future?)

13. Which rooms of the house are seen in the dream—living room, dining room, kitchen, bedroom? Which rooms are spacious and which ones are cramped? Which room contains most of the activity? Which room is unused? (List what each room is used for: what is the room's purpose? Can you relate that to part of your waking life situation? Look at the kitchen as a place of nourishment, the bathroom as a place for elimination or cleansing, the bedroom as a place for intimacy or rest, and the living room as a place for interacting with others.)

14. Are there rooms that you did not know existed? How are the rooms furnished? Are there antiques inherited from others, or is it filled with your most treasured objects? (Are

there parts of yourself that you have not discovered or are neglected?)

15. What basic systems are parts of the house? What's going on with the systems in the house—for example, the water, electricity, heater, or toilet? Is anything short-circuited? Are the toilets functioning properly to eliminate waste? Does the water for cleansing flow smoothly, or are there leaks? (Think in terms of your personal health. How are things "working" in your body?)

16. What's going on in the basement? Are you familiar with the basement area? Is there lighting installed or is it dark? Are there objects that you are not aware you had? What is the mood in the basement, and how do you feel about being in this area? (Consider the basement area as your subconscious, or where you put things that you want hidden from view.)

17. Is there an attic in your house? Were you aware that this area existed? What is stored in your attic? How do you access the area? Is it over-filled and in need of cleaning out? What do you find of interest? (The attic is often considered part of the spiritual realm of one's life, or where we store things long-term.)

18. Where is your neighborhood? What kind of location are you living in: urban, suburban, country, small town? (There is quite a difference between the feeling of a country house and that of a city building. How do you feel about your dream neighborhood?)

19. What is the relationship of the house to other houses? Is your house in harmony with its surroundings? Are other buildings and houses accessible to your house? (What is your waking relationship to others?)

20. How large is your yard? Is there a front yard (open to public view), as well as a backyard (more private area)? Is the landscape lush or barren? Are you hiding anything in your backyard? (Is part of your life hidden away from others? Are you displaying vulnerable parts of your life to people who make you feel uncomfortable, or are you safely beginning to open yourself up to others?)

Exercise: Recurring Dreams

It is helpful to note patterns of recurring themes, characters, emotions, beliefs, settings, plots, etc. Often recurring dreams come to show us that an issue needs immediate attention. The message may have been offered more subtly in the past and now you are called upon to wake up and pay attention. New understanding can be gained from any recurring information. Subtle patterns in your dreams often go unrecognized, but recurring images or themes that "drive you crazy" to pay attention are more obvious.

This exercise will help you move outside the dream and view it as an observer.

Take time to look back through your dreams and choose three or four that have occurred within a few months of each other. Recurring dream themes are especially good to use in this way.

Fill in the Recurring Dream Elements form (categories listed below; see Appendix for full-size sample), using the dreams you have chosen. Complete information from one dream, separate with a horizontal line and add information from additional dreams.

Ask the following questions:

1. Who are the recurring characters? Is there a surprise character?
2. What are the recurring settings? How do the settings relate to each other?
3. What emotions are most prominent in the dreams? Do any of them relate to your present life? Your past?
4. When do the dreams occur? Are there any similarities? Past, present, future?
5. What objects stand out? What is the significance of each?
6. Do any colors repeat in the dreams? Are all the dreams colorful? Colorless?
7. What is the theme of each dream? What are the issues of each dream? What is trying to be accomplished? What supports it being accomplished, or prevents it from being accomplished?
8. What are the belief systems that support each dream? Are they similar or conflicting?

After answering the questions, stand back and try to see if there is a recurring message for you in the series of dreams.

Wake Up ... a bit earlier each morning, remember and record your dreams, and be enlightened for the day by choosing an exercise to uncover a message from your dream maker. It's fun! Try it. I have included additional exercises in the Appendices to help you open up your dream messages.

CHAPTER 7

⊚⊚

Share and Increase the Results of Your Personal Growth

Working with dreams in groups is a far superior method of raising to consciousness and releasing the multiple creative energies, increased understandings, and gifts for living that dreams invariably bring.

—Jeremy Taylor

Are you beginning to see the dream characters that represent parts of yourself acting and reacting in various ways? Are you viewing your positive and negative characteristics—the qualities that help you move forward and the ones that prevent you from achieving personal growth? The dream is an excellent tool for this aspect of change and individuation.

If you have the tendency to blame others, you are going to find a major shift in your life when you accept responsibility for future choices.

The dream gives you a glimpse of who you really are. Remember: As you begin to visualize this more authentic way of being, you begin to act differently and then people are going to treat you differently. At this point, you have begun to grow into the person your soul yearns to be.

Others feel comfortable around people who are honest and open with their true nature. Have you taken the risk to share vulnerabilities with safe people? Try on your authentic nature around people you trust and feel will be open to your efforts.

Through dreamwork, you can gain a new confidence in your ability to know your own truth, to believe you have wisdom, and to trust that you have the tools needed to create a spiritually rewarding life.

Penny's Dream: Socrates
Emotions: nervous or anxious (AFRAID), amused (GLAD)

I'm with my husband in England and we are at a countryside train station. In the queue to get on the train, people line up in numbered seats. Some people leave, and we rush to get in the front of the line.

As we wait to get on the train, a female platform conductor (more like a ticket agent) gives us instructions. She is American and I say something in jest about coming all this way, only to get an American accent. She jokes that her specialty or religion is "Socrates."

ᘐᓎ

The Active Imagination exercise was done quickly in one of my dream circles. The answers were written with the non-dominant hand (see Chapter 6). This had an immediate, strong emotional impact for the dreamer when she read her answers aloud to the group.

1. Who are you? *I'm your extroverted self.*
2. What should I call you? *Socrates.*
3. Why are you here in my dream? *To give you a feel for performance, for being "out there" more.*
4. What do you want from me? *To step out on the platform and take your place.*
5. What do you know that I don't know? *I know that your place is reserved. It's yours. No striving is required. Just walk over.*
6. What is the most important thing that you have to tell me? *It's all in the quest; in the asking. Code word: Socrates.*

The dreamer reports: "There were many layers of meaning to this dream. The dream came at a time when I was asking "What's next" for me in my work as a therapist and dream teacher. I am in the process of finishing my creative project of Dream Oracle cards and they are based on my work on dreams in ancient Greece. Socrates is one of the cards and it represents "Soul Questions," so this dream told me that the questions I've been asking are important to my soul. In fact, the Socratic question was more important than the answer, another important feature for me. The ticket agent is on the platform and that is significant as an unpublished author. Publishers tell us, "You have to have a platform." So this dream was also telling me that I need to get my work out there and build a platform. The Platform Director was quite outgoing; something I am not in my waking life. After attending some disappointing workshops at a conference, I thought, "I can do better than that," and Socrates confirmed this in my Active Imagination as he told me to "take my place."

Encouraging Risk

You may wonder why fear is a predominant emotion of your dreams. We fear what we do not know. If dreams encourage dreamers to grow into their full potential, then that leads us into the unknown—and, therefore, into anxiety. Your dreams will nudge you to take more risks that will lead toward positive change. Look at ways in which your dreams encourage you to take risks and move into unfamiliar territory. Take risks with new behaviors in your waking life, and become aware of the successful outcome of taking those risks.

Friends and Family

Although change is an individual accomplishment, others close to us play a role by offering support and encouragement.

Just as dreams are personal and individual, so is personal growth or transformation. It is not a group accomplishment. Family members won't all achieve personal growth in the same way or on the same timetable. However, family and friends do, in many ways, encourage (or discourage) change in others.

In order to gain support and encouragement to continue your path of personal growth, you may need to show family members that you are changing by bringing to their attention that your action in a particular situation is different than it was in the past. People tend to perceive a situation as they expect it to be.

Others don't notice the change in us when they are caught up in their old reactions to us. This was a difficult realization for me. I tried so hard to make new choices and react in different ways, yet I met resistance. People who are closest to us often expect us to continue acting as we always have, and they have trouble being open to the fact that we are making conscious changes in the way we live. You may need to share with those close to you some of the things you are attempting to do and ask for their support.

Building Community through Dream Groups

It is easier to change if you feel safe. It is helpful if you have some sense that if you fail, you will not be devastated. You need a container—a place that holds you and allows you to make a shift without being afraid that you will lose yourself. Dream groups provide this support and a sense of community.

Working with dreams on an individual basis is productive and fulfilling. Working with others magnifies the rewards of the dreamwork. Your dreams are tailor-made for you, but you can gain much information for your life through the dreams of others because of the "collective unconscious" and the thread of humanity that runs through all dreams.

Groups of people gather throughout the world to form dream groups in order to share and find meaning in their nighttime dreams. The format may vary, but the goal is similar: to support each other in following the guidance offered by their dreams.

Mentally healthy people are attracted to group dreamwork as an opportunity for change and personal growth. The dream group acts as a container for the deep and difficult work of individuation, thus confidentiality and mutual respect are integral parts of effective group work. A dream group provides a safe community where people are free of being judged and can be vulnerable and honest. Sometimes a dream group is the first experience a member has of being honest and open with others.

The dream group offers a depth and breadth of communication and sharing that is found in few other gatherings. Dream groups help ease the process of change—just as the dream itself eases the process. An advantage to working on dreams within a group is that new insights and perspectives are possible that you may not have realized on your own. The group enhances the work by building community, increasing insight, encouraging new ways of being, and acting as a mirror for each member. We observe others doing their work and often get insight into our own patterns of resistance.

Members of the group offer you many ideas for action ("if it were my dream"). After all, they don't have to do the work involved to make the change! Even when we reject a particular idea because it is not what we want to do or how we want to view the situation, we are growing by identifying what we do *not* want. By saying, "I don't think that is appropriate for my life," you are more clearly defining what does and doesn't feel right.

Within a group, members can test new ways of being. It is a safe place to try out new behaviors. The group encourages the members to be more than they have ever been. All of this allows you to change and grow safely within the small community of the dream group, which then leads you to trust in the larger world.

One of my long-term group members shared these thoughts: "The group facilitates my process in many ways. It gives me a broader view, varied insight, an antidote to authoritarian structure, strength in numbers, reassurance that I am not alone. We are sharing the same desire for personal growth and the collective unconscious plays a part so that the process is softened. We can get at very difficult emotional issues. When the emotional outbursts come, it's pure support from the group!"

Join with several acquaintances and begin your own dream group. You will be glad you did! The effort required to form the group will be greatly outweighed by the rewards.

A longtime member of one of my dream groups wrote:

The dream group members are more comfortable being open and trusting. They continue to share more specifics of personal life and inner struggles. All demonstrate the courage to live with tension to make changes in their lives, acknowledging both the ups and downs inherent in every situation. The dream group members are getting to be at home with the many/ multiple parts of themselves that show up in dreams. All accept more and more responsibility in expressing their distinctive talents in unique, meaningful activities, and show more reliance on inner guidance and direction.

Organizing a Dream Group

If you are interested in organizing a dream group (and I encourage you to do so,) I have created just the book for you! *Honoring the Dream: A Handbook for Dream Group Leaders* is a helpful resource with step-by-step guidelines for creating a group and facilitating the dreamwork within the group. It's all you need to get started! You can find more information on my website, www.DreamSynergy.org

Lives Changed by Dreamwork

As you open up to your dreams, you will no longer live as you did before. You will model positive change for friends, family, and colleagues.

A longtime dream group member tells me: "Dreamwork has changed my life immensely—made me more aware of themes in my life that I want to devote energy to—made me more accepting of negative or fearful emotions—helped me to see things more clearly by using story and metaphors—guided me to a dream study group which, along with my dreams, has supported me through cancer and many other life issues with its acceptance, nurturing, and help ..."

Betty's Dream: Coming Out of the Attic
Emotions: anxious to get out, afraid of suffocation, panicked (AFRAID). Upon waking, relieved (GLAD)

I am walking down the stairs from my attic to the second story in my home, but the staircase is only about one foot wide. Awkwardly, I have to turn sideways to get down the stairs and I feel squeezed, panicky as I make my way down the dimly lit stairway to the main floor.

ɞ

Waking life: For the past two years, since earning my dreamwork certification from the Institute for Dream Studies (IDS), I have been building a business slowly, partly due to circumstances but partly out of fear of taking a big step. Just before this dream, I took advantage of an opportunity to have an office outside of my home. My office had been in my attic for the last two years.

Upon waking, I had the strong feeling that it [was] more uncomfortable to be "coming out" than it will be to "be out" in the world with my work. The metaphor of a birth canal came to me quickly. There is no going back and it will be better out than in.

Wake Up! Are you hiding out from your authentic, true, empowered potential? Do you need to come out of your "attic?" Metaphorically, what is your "attic?" Where do you hide your gifts? What do you yearn to offer the world? All humanity will benefit when you let your light shine!

CHAPTER 8

⊚⊚

Live with Awareness and Your Authentic Self!

The true spiritual secret is this: What you seek, you already are. True success is discovering your inner divinity—it's the ability to love and have compassion, trust your intuition, and awaken to your unlimited creative nature.

—Deepak Chopra

You once knew who you were. As children we know. I am reminded of an old blessing: "God bless the children, who knew the truth before they were taught otherwise." The first time I heard that, I cried. I did not know who I was until I was in my fifties. As a child, I was often reprimanded for being myself. Parents, siblings, teachers, and society offer us much, but at the same time they contribute to the loss of Self for each child.

I am remembering that person who was born to be me. It feels good; it feels right to be honestly Justina. I hope that you are getting to know your authentic Self once again. We once trusted our feelings, beliefs, creativity, and intuition. Your dreams want to lead you back to that core understanding of who you are, to know and respect your beautiful and fearless Self—the part that is able to take risks and not sabotage the results. The dream will guide, support, and cheer your renewed positive behavior. You will first get a glimpse of yourself in the dream, then you begin to act like that person, then people treat you like that, and then you move into your authentic nature—the person you desire to be!

Perhaps you can find a photo of yourself when you were a child and place it in a nice frame beside your bed. Embrace the inner child who has been waiting to be re-connected to you, to be embraced by you. Remember when you liked to play in an imaginary world for hours? When did you lose that? It is time to find those meaningful and enjoyable times again. It's time to let go of the belief that your imagination is not "real" and therefore not important.

Children know. They don't doubt what they know until they are taught to question. Using intuition is natural for a child. They make easy, quick decisions that are usually right in line with what they want and need. They know what their talents and abilities are and act accordingly. It is only when they are expected to be good at everything that they begin to question their ability to succeed at anything.

Pay attention to your inner intelligence. In our culture, intuition is undervalued. We put our emphasis on intellect. Albert Einstein said, "The intuitive mind is a sacred gift and the rational mind is a faithful servant. We have created a society that honors the servant and has forgotten the gift." Open up to your intuition during your waking life. You are going to be astonished when you recognize how "right on" you often are without the use of what you have learned in school or from books.

Do you remember who you were as a child? Do you remember what you wanted to be before you were told that it was not possible? Or maybe you were one of the few children who were not told "otherwise." Lucky you! I love seeing the determination and belief of children when I ask what they want to become. Recently, I met a dynamic, radiant young girl who said with confidence that she is going to be a "rock star." I don't doubt that she could be, but I know that she will encounter barriers and negativity to becoming all she dreams of being.

You have not lost your authentic nature. You have overridden it by your own "parental" voices. It is easy to let "shoulds" and "oughts" rule your life in many ways.

You cannot blame others anymore for keeping you from living from your full potential. We carry our own negative voices. It is our negativity—not the negativity of others—that limits us. Our dreams help us hear and identify those voices. Our dreams encourage us to quiet those voices and let positive, supportive voices be heard.

Justina's Dream: Can't Hold on to What I Am Carrying
Emotions: anxious (AFRAID), MAD, defeated (SAD)

I am carrying too much and keep dropping things. When I stoop to pick up one thing, then another thing falls out of my arms. I am tired and so "frustrated" by my inability to hold on and go where I need to go. I wonder why I don't just stop and take time to deliver some of the things so I don't have to carry them all around. It doesn't seem as if there is time for that!

ॐ

When I woke, it really hit me how much I am carrying now and in the next few months—too much! I decided that I had to stop that day and take the time to put some things "down," as well as find out how I really felt about it if "frustrated" is not a word that I find helpful in dealing with emotions. I realized that I was really "mad" at myself for letting myself get in this situation—it was time to take responsibility and action. I first made a list of what I was "carrying

---

151

around" so I could see what I was able to put down forever, and other things that I might deliver to others to "carry," then set up a schedule of "delivery times" for other things so I didn't feel like I was carrying them all at one time. Wow, it was amazing how much better I felt by the end of that day! Nothing had changed except my perspective.

Keep Your Nighttime Dreams and Your Waking Dreams Alive

In order to be successful in making significant changes in your life, you must commit to bring your dreams into your waking life. Do what you can to help keep the recent revelations at the forefront of your thoughts.

Make a commitment to your daily dreamwork. As with any aspect of life, some readers will be ready to dig in to the work and others will be doing all they want by remembering a dream every now and then.

Just like any other effort we make, "The more you put into it, the more you get out of it!" If you really want to make changes in your life, you must be willing to live the dream.

See the following suggestions to help you carry over your dreamwork to your waking life.

Eleven Reminders for Honoring Your Dreams and Your Destiny

1. Be intentional about remembering your dreams each night. Try incubating a dream question (see Chapter 2.)

2. Prepare for dreamtime each night. Always have paper and pencil, tape recorder, or phone with app ready by the bed.

3. Allow time in your morning schedule to record your dream. Set your alarm fifteen minutes earlier so there will be time for dream recall. Use the snooze button to stay quiet while you gather your dreams. Don't expect the dreams to wait for you to record them later in the day.

4. Continue to keep the dream alive during the week by reviewing your notes before bed. Continue to make connections to the dream. It is often easier to understand the message days after first recording the dream. We often have a broader perspective after some time has elapsed.

5. Connect past dreams to more recent dreams and your life. Look at your dream index. Are any of the dream titles similar? What emotions are repeating? Does anything remind you of your waking life?

6. Think of daily activities as if they occurred within a dream. Reflect on questions that might be addressed by this "waking dream."

7. Be aware of behavior during the week that relates to the dream. Be open to seeing your ways of acting and reacting to situations in life. Be open to seeing how the dream message relates to relationships, career, and health.

8. Live your dream! Practice daily being who the dream beckons you to be. In waking life, try on new ways of behaving offered by the dream. You may feel like you are "acting," since this will not be familiar behavior. If you are putting yourself in the picture for the first time, you may encounter resistance from others. Pay attention to "healthy behavior."

9. Create rituals to honor each dream. During the week, carry through with your idea to honor your dream.

10. Note the new "wisdom" from your dreams on index cards, and keep them where you can see them and reflect on them each day.

11. Join a dream group in your community or online. If there is not one to join, organize one!

Honoring Your Dreams

Take time to reread previous dreams. It is often easier to find the message days after first recording the dream.

It is up to you to live the dream in your life. Share with others (safe listeners) the impact that dreamwork is making in your life, and the changes that are happening for you.

Make sure that you are practicing the suggestions for honoring the dream each day. Making time for your personal dreamwork is your responsibility. Go ahead: lead the way, clearing a path for you, your family, and your friends. Why not the entire world!?

International Association for the Study of Dreams (IASD)

The International Association for the Study of Dreams (IASD) is a helpful and valuable organization and resource. Go to its website (www.iasdreams.org). Become a member in order to receive the publications and information provided to members. Through international conferences, you have the opportunity to get to know dreamers from all around the world, as well as learn from the IASD workshops and lectures.

Online E-study groups sponsored by IASD cover many topics of interest regarding the world of dreams. Join one!

Ripple Effect

In my research with dreamers in my long-term dream group, I found that members were surprised by how family and friends were influenced by the changes that the dreamers made in their lives. One member said, "Because I am more open and less judgmental, my children are now more open. That impacts their friends, as well. Even my husband is now interested in his dreams and is making moves toward a more authentic life—even thinking about retirement!" Another member shared that her parents are listening more closely to her since she has reclaimed her personal authority. She noticed that not only they, but also her entire family, treat her with more respect.

As Jean Shinoda Bolen describes in her book *The Millionth Circle*, "When a critical number of people change how they think and behave, the culture will also, and a new era begins."

Dreams and Creativity

I encourage you to honor the creativity expressed through your dreams.

As children, we express our creativity. Then we are taught that we are deficient. The dream shows us otherwise. ("Otherwise" is an interesting word: "wise in another way" or "wise as another might be.") The dream is never quelled by others' opinions. It continues to be a masterpiece of creativity throughout our lives.

The creative nature of dreams gives me a glimpse into my creative spirit. I am amazed that I'm creative enough to write and direct a great play with deep meaning. I am the playwright, director, producer, costume designer, characters, even the set designer for each one of my dreams. I use metaphor, simile, word association, setting, character, humor, and farce in exceptional ways—beyond my conscious capabilities.

Even though I am an artist by training, I never recognized or believed in my full creative potential until I became involved in dreamwork.

I've had many clients who are artists and have expanded their work and their creativity by paying attention to their dreams. Their way of seeing the world, their connection to it, and the ways in which they express images that represent the human experience—all of this expands immensely.

Justina's Dream: My Hands Blossom
Emotions: AFRAID, relieved (GLAD), awed (GLAD)

I am in my room and look down at my hands. Green vines are shooting out of them. It is very scary. I have never seen anything like it. It's really weird.

I show my hands to my daughters. They can't believe what they see, but act calm. I want to see a doctor!

After a while, the vines disappear: they retract and there are no signs of them on my hands.

Later, the vines come out again, but with beautiful little white blossoms! Not as scary as before since they are so pretty. Wow!

This dream came at a time when I was writing this book. I "planned" to complete it by the time of this dream, but it was taking much longer than I had imagined it would. I even began to wonder if I should be writing the book at all: "I am NOT a writer!" (I had been told this by my father so many times as I went through school. Old belief systems die hard.)

At first in this dream, Dream Ego is frightened to see this new growth (the new creative talents and abilities that emerge as we grow and change), which carries with it the responsibility to use the gifts productively. Change and personal growth are sometimes difficult to accept and in the dream I want to see a "doctor"—someone who can change it back to the way that is familiar and therefore more comfortable.

The dream gave me new hope and belief that my hands contain the creative growth (green vines) and beauty of new beginnings (white flowers) necessary to write the book. I was growing into a writer—and this was just the support I needed to continue—and enjoy!—the process of writing. (New beliefs: I am a writer and growing every day!)

Your Future Authentic Self

You are not becoming a "new" person. You are actually re-claiming your original identity and potential. You are sloughing off all the learned behaviors and beliefs that never fit who you were born to be. (Even snakes shed their skin as they grow and mature.)

Your dreams yearn for you to move to that "childlike" belief in yourself as "rock star" in whatever profession you choose. Your dreams will always be on your side, leading you to your Authentic Self. Dreams will not sabotage your waking dreams. They will support, nudge, and encourage you all the way to success and enlightenment.

You are going to enjoy being your Authentic Self. You will feel good in your new (newborn) skin. It is going to fit just right.

Linda's dream: Sock Monkey
Emotions: terrified, panicked (AFRAID)

Breathless, with my heart racing, I charge up the stairs. Higher and higher I climb the spiraling staircase, knowing my pursuer is just steps behind me. Finally I reach the top only to find myself trapped in a room full of closed doors. I can see the shadow of my pursuer growing larger as it approaches closer and closer.

Desperately I begin to scream for help as I catch the first glimpse of my attacker. Is it a monster, an evil witch, a deranged serial killer? No, worse! It's a Sock Monkey! Terrified, I beat on the doors, pleading for help, when I hear a gentle voice softly shaking me back to reality, "Wake up. Wake up. It's just a dream."

Safely back in her waking physical reality, the dreamer realized she had just been shown a well-directed and choreographed vision of her Inner Reality.

The dreamer asked herself, "Why am I so scared of a Sock Monkey?" By asking herself what is one good thing about being a Sock Monkey, she got a clue to some unrealized potential she carried. She was aware that dream characters like the Sock Monkey often chase us in the direction we need to go or to the place we need to be without doing real harm.

Since working with her "Sock Monkey" dream, she has been more aware of her ability to transform from something useful but ordinary into something playful, and also comforting. She is paying more attention to the doors of opportunity that are open to her for new growth and balancing that with playtime. She tells me she has fun and laughs a lot more. Her youngest child just graduated from college and this was a time of transition for her. Being responsible and a "good mother" often got in the way of her enjoying herself. It was a pattern in her life that separated her from those she loved. Her dreams were helping her adjust to the empty nest and her new role as mother of adult children!

Did you Wake Up? What is your intention, and what is your commitment to your dreams?

Now go out and share yourself with the world. Spread the power of dreams and the freedom of moving back to your God-given wonderful being. Claim your talents and abilities that have been hidden. Begin to do those things you enjoy—not the things that satisfied your parents or teachers. Live your life in a way that embodies your chosen beliefs and values.

Welcome to the world—once again! This is who you were born to be!

Epilogue

My dream for you is that ...

... you are inspired to honor your dreams in a new, more respectful way.

... you will accept all the parts of yourself, your emotions and your new beliefs.

... you have moved beyond the limiting rational mind and have limitless faith that you can have the kind of life that you dream of.

... you believe in yourself in new adventurous ways.

... you are creating a waking life that is filled with wonder, awe and joy.

... you will embrace your authentic self and live the full and unique life that you were born to live.

Glossary

anima, animus

Jung refers to the archetypes of the soul as the animus and the anima. Animus encompasses traits that are "masculine"—that is, more outward-directed and concerned with going out into the world and doing. Anima embraces personality aspects that are "feminine"—more inner-directed and concerned with being comfortable with emotions, people, and creative energy.

Everyone possesses both animus and anima, but generally speaking we are not conscious of them. It is helpful in our journey to wholeness to balance these aspects of our personality.

The dream is particularly well suited to making us aware of unconscious anima/animus material, thereby facilitating our personal development.

archetypes

Underlying patterns that form the basic blueprint for the major dynamic components of the human personality. They are part of our inheritance as members of the human race. Jung explains the archetype as "an inherited tendency of the human mind to form representations of mythological motifs—representations that vary a great deal without losing their basic pattern." Examples include Mother or Father, Devil, Goddess, Lover, etc.

belief system

A preset, consistent (often unconscious) set of beliefs prevailing in a family, community, or society.

core issue

A central and major psychological matter that usually derives from childhood experiences and deters a person from moving forward in personal growth.

gestalt

A form of psychology popularized by psychologist Fritz Perls. The work, which is usually done in groups, focuses on attempts to broaden a person's awareness of Self by using past experiences, memories, emotional states, and bodily sensations. Gestalt work encourages the person to act out painful situations and reintegrate the disowned parts into his current life. Techniques include empty chair conversations, dialogue, exaggeration of behavior, staying with feelings, dialogues with self, etc. Dreamwork is an important aspect of Gestalt work.

image

A mental representation of something. If I dream about the house I lived in as a child, that is an image; if I dream about the house in which I currently live, that is both an image and an aspect of my waking reality. In both cases the image represents ideas beyond the meaning of "house." In the first case, perhaps the place where I "grew up" or "learned family scripts"; in the second, possibly "the way I live now" or "where I now feel at home."

incubation

A practice used by ancient Greeks and other cultures to arrive at answers to important questions. Today we use dream incubation for similar purposes. It consists of being intentional about a request for an answer to a specific question. Before going to bed the dreamer prepares his/her specific question, writes it on paper, and then contemplates the question as he/she is going to sleep. Often with this intentionality the dreamer awakens with a clear answer.

individuation

A term used by Carl Jung to describe the personal process of moving toward wholeness and completion, or to the true "Self." It is a process of integrating various parts of yourself (ego, conscious, and unconscious), becoming closer to your authentic being and the person you were born to be. Through individuation, human beings are differentiated from other human beings.

Jung, Carl Gustav (1875 –1961)

A Swiss psychiatrist who developed analytical psychology. He created and developed the concepts of extraversion, introversion, synchronicity, and the collective unconscious. His work has been very influential in psychiatry, religion, philosophy, anthropology, and literature. Jung regarded individuation as the central process of human development.

lucid dreaming

The dreamer awakens fully within the dream and can contribute to the outcome of the dream by becoming consciously involved. During lucid dreaming, everything seems bright and clear, and the senses are heightened. Lucid dreaming is sometimes used to practice new forms of behavior.

metaphor

An image or symbol that represents a larger concept. For example, in a dream the action of crossing the street might represent the idea of "crossing over" from one way of seeing and doing things to a different or opposite way of seeing and doing things.

passive-aggressive behavior

A display of aggression that is indirect as opposed to direct. Passive-aggressive conduct might take the form of such behaviors as being habitually late, forgetting or failing to keep agreements, carelessness in carrying out agreed-upon tasks, etc. The person exhibiting this type of behavior is expressing aggression passively rather than actively.

projection

The unconscious act or process of ascribing to another person one's own ideas, impulses, or emotions, especially when they are considered undesirable or cause anxiety.

psyche

The Greeks envisioned the psyche as the soul or the very essence of life. More conventionally, "psyche" is thought of as "the mind."

REM (rapid eye movement)

Most dreaming occurs during this stage of sleep characterized by rapid eye movements. In this period of sleep the pulse rate quickens, breathing becomes irregular, and large muscles are limp. We are basically paralyzed during this period of sleep.

self

Webster's definition of self (pertaining to our ego-self) is "the identity, character, or essential qualities of any person or thing." Carl Jung introduced the word Self (using a capital S to denote the difference from the ego-self) to refer to a "supra-ordinate, inner, unknown, divine center of the psyche which we have to explore all our lifetime."

I believe that one's true nature—that is, the authentic Self—is the person that one is born to be: in other words, one's God-given nature. It is not influenced by outside factors. I use this idea as a working definition for the role of self in the process of change.

symbol

An object or image that represents something else by association, resemblance, or convention. Symbols have both personal and universal meanings.

synchronicity

The occurrence of two or more events perceived as meaningfully related, although the events might not occur simultaneously. The events might be perceived as a meaningful coincidence rather than causally related. The concept of synchronicity was first described by Carl Jung.

unconscious

A domain of the psyche encompassing repressed functions, primitive impulses and desires, memories, images, and wishes that are too anxiety-provoking to be accepted into consciousness. Although the individual is not conscious of the material of the unconscious, it influences his/her emotions and behavior.

tension of the opposites

Jung taught that if the tension between two opposing forces can be held independently without yielding to the urge to identify with one or the other, then an unexpected third force might emerge which will unite the opposing forces in a new, creative way.

Suggested Reading

Andrews, Ted (1993). *Animal-Speak: The Spiritual & Magical Powers of Creatures Great & Small*. Llewllyn Publications.

Barasch, Marc (2000). *Healing Dreams: Exploring the Dreams That Can Transform Your Life*. Riverhead Books.

Barrett, Deirdre, and Patrick McNamara (2012). *Encyclopedia of Sleep and Dreams: The Evolution, Function, Nature, and Mysteries of Slumber*. Greenwood Press.

Bethards, B. (1983). *The Dream Book: Symbols for Self-Understanding*. Inner Light Foundation.

Bolen, Jean Shinoda (1999). *The Millionth Circle: How to Change Ourselves and the World*. Conari Press.

Bosnak, Robert (2007). *Embodiment: Creative Imagination in Medicine, Art and Travel*. Routledge

Bulkeley, Kelly (1997). *An Introduction to the Psychology of Dreaming*. Praeger Publishers.

Bulkeley, Kelly (2000). *Transforming Dreams: Learning Spiritual Lessons from the Dreams You Never Forget*. John Wiley & Sons.

Bulkeley, Kelly, and Rev. Patricia Bulkeley (2005). *Dreaming Beyond Death: A Guide to Pre-Death Dreams and Visions*. Beacon Press.

Bulkeley, Kelly, and Alan Siegel (1998). *Dreamcatching: Every Parent's Guide to Exploring and Understanding Children's Dreams and Nightmares*. Three Rivers Press.

Campbell, Jean (2006). *Group Dreaming: Dreaming to the Tenth Power*. Wordminder Press.

Campbell, Joseph (1968). *The Hero with a Thousand Faces* (2nd edition). Princeton University Press.

Campbell, Joseph (1970). *Myths, Dreams and Religion*. E.P. Dutton.

Dalfen, Layne (2002). *Dreams Do Come True: Decoding Your Dreams to Discover Your Full Potential*. Adams Media Corporation.

Delaney, Gayle (1998). *All About Dreams: Everything You Need to Know About Why We Have Them, What They Mean, and How to Put Them to Work for You*. Harper San Francisco.

Emery, Marcia (1994). *Dr. Marcia Emery's Intuition Workbook: An Expert's Guide to Unlocking the Wisdom of Your Subconscious Mind*. Prentice Hall.

Garfield, Patricia (2003). *Dream Catcher: A Young Person's Journal for Exploring Dreams*. Tundra Books.

Gordon, David (2006). *Mindful Dreaming: A Practical Guide for Emotional Healing through Transformative Mythic Journeys*. New Page Books.

Gratton, Nicole (1998). *Les Rêves, Messagers De La Nuit*. Les Éditions de l'Homme. Available as Amazon eBook titled *Dream Incubation* (2014).

Gratton, Nicole, and Monique Sequin (2014). *Dreams and Death: The Benefits of Dreams Before, During and After Death*. Translated from the French by Micheline Vallee Turp (Kindle version).

Hartmann, Ernest (2000). *Dreams and Nightmares: The Origin and Meaning of Dreams*. Perseus Publishing.

Hill, Clara E. (1996). *Working with Dreams in Psychotherapy*. The Guilford Press.

Hoss, Robert (1996). *Dream Language: Self-Understanding through Imagery and Color*. Innersource.

Irwin, Lee (2007). *Alchemy of Soul: The Art of Spiritual Transformation*. Lorian Press.

Johnson, Robert A. (1986). *Inner Work: Using Dreams and Active Imagination for Personal Growth*. Harper & Row.

Johnson, Robert A. (1991). *Owning Your Own Shadow: Understanding the Dark Side of the Psyche.* Harper & Row.

Jung, C.G. (1985). *Memories, Dreams, Reflections.* Vintage Books.

Jung, C.G. (1964). *Man and His Symbols.* Doubleday & Company.

Kahn, David L. (2007). *A Dream Come True: Simple Techniques for Dream Interpretation and Precognitive Dream Recognition.* Cosimo, Inc.

King, Phil, Kelly Bulkeley and Bernard Welt (2011). *Dreaming in the Classroom.* State University of New York Press.

Krippner, Stanley, and J. Dillard (1988). *Dreamworking: How to Use Your Dreams for Creative Problem-Solving.* Bearly Limited.

Krippner, Stanley, and Mark Waldman (Editor) (1999). *Dreamscaping: New Techniques for Understanding Yourself and Others.* Lowell House.

Krippner, Stanley, and David Feinstein (2008). *Personal Mythology: Using Ritual, Dreams, and Imagination to Discover your Inner Story* (3rd edition). Energy Psychology Press/Elite Books.

Krippner, Stanley, and Stephen Kierulff (2004). *Becoming Psychic: Spiritual Lessons for Focusing Your Hidden Abilities.* New Page Books.

Lasley, Justina (2004). *Honoring the Dream: A Handbook for Dream Group Leaders.* DreamsWork.

Lesser, Elizabeth (2000). *The Seeker's Guide: Making Your Life a Spiritual Adventure.* Villard Books.

Lyons, Tallulah (2012). *Dreams and Guided Imagery: Gifts for Transforming Illness and Crisis.* Balboa Press.

Mallon, Brenda (2000). *Dreams, Counseling and Healing.* Gill & MacMillan.

Mallon, Brenda (2002). *Dream Time with Children: Learning to Dream, Dreaming to Learn.* Jessica Kingsley Publishers.

Metcalf, Linda Trichter, and Tobin Simon (2002). *Writing the Mind Alive: The Proprioceptive Method for Finding Your Authentic Voice.* Ballantine Books.

Moss, Robert (1996). *Conscious Dreaming: A Spiritual Path for Everyday Life*. Three Rivers Press.

Norment, Rachel G (2013). *A Journey in Self-Knowledge and Self-Realization*. Balboa Press.

Raffa, Jean Benedict (2012). *Healing the Sacred Divide: Making Peace with Ourselves, Each Other and the World*. Larson Publications.

Raffa, Jean Benedict (1994). *Dream Theatres of the Soul: Empowering the Feminine through Jungian Dream Work*. Innisfree Press, Inc

Russo, Richard (1987). *Dreams Are Wiser Than Men*. Publishing Group West.

Siegel, Alan (2003). *Dream Wisdom: Uncovering Life's Answers in Your Dreams*. Celestial Arts.

Strickling, Bonnelle (2007). *Dreaming About the Divine*. State University of New York Press.

Tanner, Wilda (1988). *The Mystical, Magical, Marvelous World of Dreams*. Sparrow Hawk Press.

Taylor, Jeremy (2009). *The Wisdom of Your Dreams: Using Dreams to Tap into Your Unconscious and Transform Your Life*. Jeremy P. Tarcher/Penguin.

Taylor, Jeremy (1998). *The Living Labyrinth: Exploring Universal Themes in Myths, Dreams, and the Symbolism of Waking Life*. Paulist Press.

Ullman, Montague (1996). *Appreciating Dreams: A Group Approach*. Sage Publications.

Ullman, Montague, and Nan Zimmerman (1979). *Working with Dreams*. J.P. Tarcher.

Van de Castle, Robert (1994). *Our Dreaming Mind*. Ballantine Books.

Von Franz, Marie-Louise (1991). *Dreams: A Study of the Dreams of Jung, Descartes, Socrates, and Other Historical Figures*. Shambhala Publications.

Waggoner, Robert (2008). *Lucid Dreaming: Gateway to the Inner Self.* Moment Point Press.

☺/☺

**Additional dream-related books are listed at
www.asdreams.org/subidxshopbooks_members.htm**

Index

transformation 15, 21, 59, 62, 76, 77,
    85, 132, 143, 170, 199
transpersonal xvi, 46, 199
transportation 67
triangles 133
trickster archetype 52
trinity 65
Twist, Lynne and Bill 4

U

Ullman, Montague 128, 172
unconscious xvii, 3, 6, 7, 20, 26, 27,
    32, 36, 40, 42, 48, 52, 53, 54, 62,
    63, 75, 100, 102, 108, 109, 116,
    119, 144, 146, 163, 165, 166, 167,
    172, 185, 186
universal symbols 36, 37, 38, 39, 40,
    46, 59, 62, 65, 75, 167
urge to change 15

V

vehicles 16
vitamin B-6 26, 185
Vocabulary of Emotions 33, 90, 91,
    96, 129, 184

W

waking-life experience (treating as
    dream) xi, xii, xvii, xxiii, xxvi,
    xxviii, 2, 3, 7, 10, 11, 20, 21, 22,
    25, 26, 27, 28, 34, 42, 46, 61, 64,
    67, 69, 71, 72, 76, 78, 80, 81, 83,
    84, 86, 87, 88, 89, 97, 98, 99,
    103, 104, 105, 106, 115, 116, 117,
    118, 119, 120, 122, 123, 125, 127,
    129, 130, 132, 134, 135, 136, 137,
    138, 143, 147, 150, 152, 153, 157,
    158, 161, 164, 185, 186, 193, 194,
    196
wallet 59
wasps 88
water xvii, 12, 13, 26, 40, 52, 53, 54,
    58, 62, 63, 72, 75, 77, 115, 117,
    138, 185
weddings 83
whale 52, 53, 54
What Are My Beliefs? (exercise) 114
What do you Choose to Believe?
    (exercise) 114, 119
What is Keeping Me Stuck? (exercise)
    194
Who am I Becoming? (exercise) 134
wholeness 19, 48, 51, 66, 163, 165
witch 50, 158

Appendices

DREAM SYNERGY

Vocabulary of Emotions

+ GLAD -	+ SAD -	+ MAD -	+ AFRAID -
amusement	alienation	agitation	anxious
appreciation	boredom	angry	awe
awe	concern	annoyance	cautious
blissful	depression	anxious	concern
calm	devastation	betrayal	confusion
confident	disappointment	bitter	defensive
content	discouragement	confusion	desperate
delight	disgrace	critical	distress
ecstatic	dismal	deception	doubtful
energetic	defeat	disgust	embarrass
enthusiastic	distraught	dismay	frustration
excitement	exhaustion	displeasure	guilty
fortunate	hopeless	domination	helpless
fulfillment	hurt	enrage	hesitant
grateful	inadequate	envious	hopeless
happy	lonely	frustration	impatient
hopeful	gloomy	hostile	insecure
joyful	guilty	humiliation	intimidation
loving	miserable	impatient	jealous
OK	mournful	irritable	lonely
optimistic	neglect	jealous	nervous
passionate	regretful	offensive	overwhelm
relaxation	rejection	rage	regretful
relief	shame	rebellious	reluctant
respect	unhappy	repulsion	suspicious
secure	unlovable	resentful	timid
sensual	invalidation	ridicule	uncertain
spiritual	upset	sabotage	uncomfortable
thankful	weary	vindictive	vulnerable
tranquil	worthless	vengeful	worry

DREAM SYNERGY

Top Ten Tips for Remembering Your Dreams

1. Acquire a dream journal in order to manifest your intention to remember your dreams and your commitment to record them.

2. Get to bed a little earlier than usual. It is helpful to feel fully rested.

3. Avoid taking unnecessary medications before bed. Antihistamines and certain other medications can inhibit recall. Vitamin B6 and the herb Mugwort are thought to increase recall.

4. Before going to bed, put your recording materials (paper and pencil) by your bed and ask your unconscious to share a dream with you during the night.

5. Before sleep, open your journal to a new page, record the date and write a brief synopsis of your day.

6. If you wake in the night, focus on any dream images you have. Jot down a few words to jog your memory in the morning. Don't let your sleepiness talk you into believing that you will remember in the morning or that the images have no significance. It is easy to talk yourself out of the steps necessary for recall.

7. Some people find it helpful to drink extra water before bed so that they have to get up in the night, thus waking up just after a REM cycle and achieving recall.

8. Upon waking, resume the sleeping position you were in while dreaming—usually your most comfortable sleeping position. This is a very successful tool. Try it!

9. If you have had no recall during the night and you cannot make any connections to your dreams upon waking, stay quietly in bed, eyes closed, and imagine some of the people in your life or some of the settings that are familiar to you. Sometimes just flipping through these images will stimulate a memory of a dream.

10. Write anything you remember—even if it is only one word, an emotion, or a physiological response. One word can sometimes lead you to important information. If you awake with a song or poem in mind, write it down. Nothing is insignificant. If you cannot remember anything, make a note to that effect in your journal. "I do not remember anything about my dreams last night." The process of writing often brings my dream back to memory. It's amazing how receptive your unconscious is to your true efforts.

DREAM SYNERGY

Guidelines for Journaling Your Dreams

1. Keep paper and pencil by your bed. You may want to use a lighted pen, keep a small flashlight nearby, or keep your eyes closed as you make notes. A pencil is dependable since it will write as long as it has a point, unlike a pen, which requires being held in a certain way for the ink to flow.

2. Tape-recording your dreams is an option. Keep a sound-activated tape recorder by your bed. Make sure it is ready to record before going to bed.

3. When you waken slightly during the night, you may write a detailed account of the dream or just a few key words. Usually some key words will jog your memory in the morning. You will be rewarded by writing down as much of the dream in the night as you can recall. The way you phrase the dream in the night is often helpful in uncovering important information.

4. Upon waking, lie still with your eyes closed and review the night's dreams. Resume your favored sleeping position, which is probably also your favorite dreaming position. Once you enter linear thinking—for example, reviewing activities scheduled for the day ahead—your dream world is left behind. It is usually very difficult to retrieve dreams once you "hit the floor."

5. Immediately transfer your dream notes to your journal either by hand or on the computer. At this time fill in any details that are missing from your night notes. It is important to do this upon first waking because your dream experience fades quickly.

6. When recording your dream, write it in the present tense, as if it's happening right now. For example, "I am standing on a cliff watching a tidal wave approach." That makes it easier to re-enter the action, emotions, and energy of the dream.

7. Separate the dream text—or what actually happens in the dream—from your waking thoughts about what you dreamed. You can make connections to your waking life later, after you've recorded the dream.

8. You may want to include the following information in your dream journal. (Your personality will determine how you choose to record your dreams.)
   - Write the date and your location.
   - Write the narrative of the dream story, with as much detail as possible. Describe the characters, setting, conversations, incidents, colors, and emotions.
   - Do not make personal connections to your life at this point—write only the dream story.
   - Create a title for your dream. Don't get caught up in giving a title. Just jot down the first thing that comes to mind. It will provide an easy handle for use in the future.
   - Identify the basic emotions of the dream. How did you feel in the dream?
   - Describe any physiological symptoms you experienced as you recorded your dream; for example, "My stomach cramped," "I felt nauseated." Note the part of the dream you were recording when you experienced these symptoms.
   - If you did not write a synopsis of the previous day's activities on the previous night, add one now. This will be very helpful later when you go back to

work a dream. (Add this information after you have recorded the dream so it doesn't interfere with your recall.)

- Draw sketches of any parts of your dream. Drawings help you understand the meaning of your dreams and take you back into the dream easily.
- Immediately note associations that come to you. Leave space to work in more depth on your dream at a later time.

9. Make an index in the back of your journal. For each dream, list the date, title and basic emotions. This makes it easier to find themes in your dreams.

ⓔ⊚

You are on your way when you begin journaling your dreams. Once you get in the habit, it will be such an adventure. You are the writer, producer, director, set and costume designer, and actors. Are you amazed at your creative genius?

DREAM SYNERGY

Recurring Dream Elements		Characters	Setting	Time	Issue/Theme	Objects	Color	Emotions

INTERNATIONAL

International Association for the Study of Dreams

To support your journey into the land of dreams, I encourage you to join the International Association for the Study of Dreams (IASD). It will educate and involve you in a community of other persons throughout the world who are interested in dreams.

What is IASD?

The International Association for the Study of Dreams is a nonprofit, international, multidisciplinary organization. Its purposes are to promote an awareness and appreciation of dreams in both professional and public arenas; to encourage research into the nature, function, and significance of dreaming; to advance the application of the study of dreams; and to provide a forum for the eclectic and interdisciplinary exchange of ideas and information.

Visit IASD's website, www.IASDreams.org, to learn more about the organization and its programs. The website is also an excellent resource for dream-related information, including articles, book suggestions, graduate programs, and more.

Who are Members of IASD?

IASD is open to anyone interested in dreams. Members come from many countries, and bring a broad range of interests, including individual and group dreamwork, academic studies, the arts, sleep research, and clinical practice. A variety of perspectives is represented among IASD's members, many of whom work in fields such as anthropology, psychology, art, history, medicine, education, literature, sociology, religion and spirituality.

IASD Programs and Publications

IASD holds an annual conference which offers a wide selection of events, including papers, panels, experiential workshops, film and art presentations, as well as the opportunity to meet and talk with scholars and researchers in many areas of dream studies. Visit www.IASDreams.org for information about, or to register for, upcoming conferences and other events.

IASD also sponsors a web-based Psiber Conference as well as Regional Meetings on a variety of dream-related topics. These meetings provide opportunities for both online and local networking among members, and educate the general public about the importance of dreams and dreamwork.

IASD publishes *Dreaming*, a quarterly, refereed, professional journal as well as *Dream Time*, which features articles on all aspects of dreaming, from the latest research on dreams to personal explorations of dream experience. Each issue includes regular review columns on dream-related books, films and websites, as well as announcements of upcoming events, calls for research, letters to the editor, and IASD news.

How do I Join?

To join, go to www.IASDreams.org, or write to IASD, P.O Box 1592, Merced, CA 95341-1592, USA, or phone 209-724-0889.

DREAM SYNERGY

Additional Dream Exercises to Explore

Select and Redefine Nouns

This was the first exercise I created to help me understand the language and the meaning of my dreams. Though time-consuming, this exercise is very powerful in helping you to understand how images represent aspects of yourself or situations in your waking life.

1. Look back over the written dream and make a vertical list of all the nouns in the dream—down the left side of the page.
2. Beside each noun, put three descriptive words or very short phrases. For example, beside "cat" you might write, "curious, quiet, independent, aloof;" beside "car" you might write, "freedom, gets me where I want to go, dependable."
3. Rewrite the entire dream using the descriptive words rather than the nouns. It may be necessary to use a phrase such as "A situation that is," "The part of myself that is," or "A place that is."

Do not to get caught up in "doing it right," but focus on uncovering meaning and new understanding.

Find the Teacher

Looking at characters in the dream as teachers or mentors is helpful in promoting personal growth. The mentors offer us new ways of looking at life and at the opportunities afforded us. This exercise is a quick way to get to an important lesson the dream has to offer.

Move into the dream as in previous exercises. Approach one dream character—a person or an animal—and ask the following questions:

1. Who are you?
2. Where did you come from?
3. Why are you here?
4. Who do you think I am?
5. What can you teach me?
6. How can I best learn what you have to teach me?

What Is Keeping Me Stuck?

Write a brief synopsis of the dream and answer the following questions.

1. What is going on emotionally in the dream?
2. What is really happening in the dream? Compare this to your current waking life.
3. What in life do you fear the most?
4. What keeps you stuck in your life?

5. How does that prevent you from moving forward in your life?

6. What would you do if there were no limits in your life? Write the answer on an index card to keep in daily view.

Individual Collage

Working with collage moves the dream to a deeper visual and emotional level. It allows you to look at the dream in a new way. The images of the collage will, of course, not create an exact replication of the dream image since the collage will be made from available pictures. Often a dream image is understood in a new way when it is represented through a similar image. Your perspective widens as you move beyond the dream image to "this picture reminds me of my dream" or "this picture reminds me of the feeling of my dream."

1. Gather a blank piece of paper, scissors, and glue. In addition to magazine and calendar photographs, you might use three-dimensional objects such as lace, buttons, or yarn.

2. Reread your dream, then close your eyes and visualize your dream before beginning the collage. Remember that this collage is to be a representation—not a replica—of the dream. Use your intuition and naturally creative Self!

3. Place your collage where you will see it often at home or your office so that you will continue to gain new insight and amplification of the dream.

Relate Dream to Waking Life

It is important to relate the dream to your waking life in each exercise you use. This brief exercise can be used quickly to tap into your dream.

1. Close your eyes and remember the action, characters, setting, and emotion of your dream.
2. Make a vertical list of images, actions, and emotions of the dream; beside each of these terms, note any waking life relationships or associations that come to mind that relate to each of the dream elements.

Journal about any insight gained.

Title Entitlement

You can gain a new perspective by looking at only the titles you have assigned your dreams.

1. Make a list of the titles of the past month's dreams.
2. Do you see any patterns or themes?
3. Read them aloud to someone else. Do they see any patterns?
4. What can you learn?

A Look at Past Dreams

Often it is easier to work with past dreams. The distance of time seems to give you a new perspective.

1. Choose a dream that is at least a month old.
2. Reread the dream aloud.
3. Do you hear any new messages?

Journal!

About the Author

Justina Lasley, MA, is the Founder and Director of the Institute for Dream Studies, an internationally recognized program that promotes the understanding of dreams and their value in helping people claim their uniqueness and full potential. She is the creator of DreamSynergy™, a comprehensive process with proven results for uncovering dream meaning, leading to personal transformation.

Justina is the author of *Honoring the Dream: A Handbook for Dream Group Leaders, In My Dream … a creative dream journal*, and this new book, *Wake Up! Use Your Nighttime Dreams to Make Your Daytime Dreams Come True*. She frequently is featured on television and radio, and in numerous newspaper and magazine articles. She is in demand as a speaker, trainer, and coach, and conducts dream groups and workshops throughout the US and abroad, at such venues as Omega Institute and the NY Open Center.

Justina's twenty years of study and practical experience expand her capabilities as an instructor and enable her to coach individuals successfully on their path of personal growth. Justina shares with clients her enthusiasm, keen insight, and talent for relating to others, facilitating their rapid movement toward a more authentic, spiritual, and fulfilling life.

Justina holds a Master's degree in Transpersonal Psychology with an emphasis in Dream Studies from the University of West Georgia, and a B.A. in both Applied Art and Education from Converse College. She also studied at the University of Paris, Parsons School of Design, and Pacifica Institute.

Justina is married to Chad Minifie and between them they have seven daughters. They reside in the Lowcountry of South Carolina, in both Charleston and Hilton Head Island.

Also by Justina Lasley

Honoring the Dream: A Handbook for Dream Group Leaders

Honoring the Dream focuses on two vital aspects of group dreamwork: the practicalities of organizing and facilitating group work, and dreamwork methods. *Honoring the Dream* shares the benefits of Justina Lasley's 14 years of experience as a dream group leader. Blending her insights about the dream with the practicalities of group work, this handbook offers step-by-step descriptions of 40 individual and group "exercises" that will mine the gold of the dream, plus 13 full-size, ready-to-use forms and handouts.

> *An international grassroots dream movement has taken hold.*
> *Justina Lasley's remarkable book,* **Honoring the Dream,** *gives*
> *leaders of dream groups a practical and authoritative manual*
> *providing guidelines that protect the dreamer's privacy and*
> *safety, without sacrificing the adventure and excitement that*
> *group dreamwork can generate.*
>   **Stanley Krippner,** Ph.D., Professor of Psychology, Saybrook
>   Graduate School; co-author *of Extraordinary*
>   *Dreams and How to Use Them*

In My Dream ... a creative dream journal

This dream journal offers a creative, instructive, useful, and informative format for recording your dreams. Use it as an adventure to follow the Dreamer within you and to become your authentic "Self" through the help of your dreams.

The journal includes hints for increasing dream recall, recording your dreams, finding meaning in your dreams, and identifying your emotions. It also has suggested readings and an index to catalogue your dreams.

> In My Dream ... *offers a way for you to capture the creative richness and insights that float up nightly from the mysterious world inside. I've written my dreams down for years, but rarely have I had such a lovely place in which to collect them. Justina Lasley's wise advice for working with dreams and Brian Andreas's magical illustrations set this dream journal apart.*
> **Sue Monk Kidd,** author of *The Mermaid Chair* and *The Secret Life of Bees*

◉◉

To purchase any of Justina Lasley's books or for information on her speaking engagements or appearances, please visit:
www.DreamSynergy.org